The Hostile Mind

THE SOURCES AND CONSEQUENCES

OF RAGE AND HATE

BY *Leon J. Saul*, M.D.

*Professor of Clinical Psychiatry and
Chief of the Section of Preventive Psychiatry,
University of Pennsylvania School of Medicine
Psychiatric Consultant to Swarthmore College*

WITH THE EDITORIAL ASSISTANCE
OF *Joan Younger*

RANDOM HOUSE · NEW YORK

FIRST PRINTING

© *Copyright, 1956, by Leon J. Saul*

All rights reserved under International and
Pan-American Copyright Conventions
Published in New York by Random House, Inc.,
and simultaneously in Toronto, Canada, by
Random House of Canada, Limited

Library of Congress Catalog Card Number: 56-5225

MANUFACTURED IN THE UNITED STATES OF AMERICA

TO

the members of the Section of Preventive Psychiatry and of the Social Hostilities Seminar at the University of Pennsylvania

FOREWORD

THE PURPOSE of this book is to provide some basic psychiatric information about human hostility. It is also a call to the relevant sciences and to intelligent men and women everywhere to turn their attention to the world's most important and urgent danger: man's hostility to man, in the hope of helping to handle, control and alleviate the great suffering it creates.

As this is written, the newspapers report that plans for a rocket trip to the moon are being discussed, that a scientist has devised a reasonable and practical way to travel to Mars and back. What was unthinkable yesterday becomes tomorrow's reality.

The fact that great strides are daily being made in the understanding of human nature rarely makes headlines. But it is true that the dream of man maturing fully, living peacefully with his fellow men, and achieving his real nature of goodness and strength is now as much within our reach *theoretically* as is the dream of space travel. What makes criminals and great men, what makes the loftiest achievements of the human spirit and what makes the destruction, chaos and unutterable bestiality and misery of war—this is now known. To apply such knowledge is a vast and enormously difficult task in human engineering, but it is only a practical task. To show that this is so and to focus attention upon it is the goal of this book.

Dr. Thoburn R. Snyder, Jr. and Mrs. Dorothy C. Selby gave unstintingly of their time in the early stages of the manuscript, Dr. Snyder in constructively critical reading of each chapter as well as preparing the index, and Mrs. Selby in editorial organization of the material.

The thanks and appreciation of the author go to his friends and associates for their constant cheerful stimulation and help; to Dr. Kenneth Appel for his unfailing support; to Dr. Edward Strecker and Dr. Lauren Smith for their constructive comments on portions of the manuscript; to Mark Riukin for his valuable suggestions; to Elizabeth (Mrs. Robert E.) Dodge and Katharine (Mrs. Edmund W.) Taylor for the typing; to Dr. William A. Jeffers for his important help, Drs. John W. Lyons, M. Royden Astley, William T. Lhamon and Mr. and Mrs. I. Edward Master for their constant understanding and good will; and to my wife and children for their critical realism and indulgent patience.

Certain of the chapters are based upon articles which appeared in technical journals, and for permission to publish these revised versions thanks are extended to *The Psychoanalytic Quarterly, The Proceedings of the American Philosophical Society* and *The American Journal of Psychiatry.*

CONTENTS

FOREWORD AND ACKNOWLEDGMENTS — vii

Part One: Biological Orientation

1. What Hostility Is — 3
2. How Hostility Arises Biologically — 9
3. The Fight-Flight Reflex Today — 16

Part Two: Basic Sources of Hostility

4. Hostility as a Disease — 27

Part Three: Hostilodynamic Mechanisms

5. How We Handle Our Hostilities — 65

Part Four: Hostility and Everyday Living

6. Hostility and Politics — 121
7. Hostility and Religion — 138
8. Hostility and Happiness — 150

Part Five: Cure and Prevention

      9. Hostility Begins at Home   163

      10. Fighting the Devil and Seeking the Grail   181

      11. Looking Forward   192

    REFERENCES   200

    INDEX   205

Part One

BIOLOGICAL

ORIENTATION

On Seeing Weather-beaten Trees

"Is it with us as clearly shown
 By slant and twist, which way
  the wind hath blown?"

ADELAIDE CRAPSEY

1 *What Hostility Is*

All words signifying emotion present difficulties of definition. They require not merely intellectual comprehension but emotional realization; that is, they have to be felt as well as understood. We have all had the experience of reading something easily, simply, and then years later understanding what it really was all about, what it really meant. And anyone who has had some psychoanalysis knows the dramatic differences between the first intellectual awareness of some psychological force and the later, emotional impact of true insight into and appreciation of it.

As to hostility, happy is he who has suffered so little from his own hates and angers and from the attacks of his fellow men that he requires a "feeling" definition. What we mean by hostility in this book is the tendency of an organism to do something harmful to another organism or to itself. It is not just aggression: aggression (from the Latin, meaning moving actively) may have a constructive meaning (as in getting a good job done); it need not be hostile, and, conversely, hostility need not be aggressive; it may be passively expressed.

Nor is hostility anger, necessarily, for anger reflects a transient feeling which can be compatible with love.

One can fully, without interruption and alteration, love someone despite periods of anger, as every husband, wife, child, parent and friend knows.

Hostility can be hate; hate expresses hostility and something deeper than anger. Hate, like hostility, implies hurt to others, expresses enmity and seeks directly no socially constructive end. There can be hostility without hate. Hate is one kind of hostility.

Hostility can take almost limitless forms, can be used for every sort of purpose, and can range in intensity from a glance or a breath of gossip to vindictiveness, violence, brutality and murder.

For hostility is the essential evil in people. Wrongness in personal and social behavior might well be judged by this touchstone: Is it *for* life, for the development, adjustment, happiness and fulfillment of society and its individuals, or is it against it?

As a technical definition one might hazard the following: Hostility is a motivating force—an impulse, urge, tendency, intent, motivation or reaction—toward injury or destruction of some kind or degree, toward an object which can be animate (including oneself) or inanimate, usually accompanied in humans by the feeling or emotion of anger; the hostility can be conscious or unconscious. As we shall see, even a single-celled animal, like the ameba, can have hostility in the sense of a reaction of destructiveness against threats and irritants to it.

It has always been important to understand the motives by which we live, love, reproduce—and hate. But today, with the finding of new, unlimitable forces of energy, it is particularly important. For today we stand

What Hostility Is

at an historic crossroads; in one discovery—the discovery of nuclear energy—we have found the means by which we can, on the one hand, destroy ourselves as a species, or, on the other, literally create a land of milk and honey, of health and happiness, a veritable heaven on earth the like of which man has never seen before.

Which choice we make depends on each of us. Human behavior has become the key to survival or to total destruction. Each individual in our society is activated by strong asocial and antisocial motivations, as well as by social ones. Only by understanding these two sets of motives, the one against life, and the other for it, can we implement those that are prohuman and reduce those that are antihuman; only in this way can we avoid the terror, tyranny, war and want that threaten us all.

All this seems clear enough on the surface, but there will be those who will resist understanding it none the less. For as well as the difficulty of understanding emotional terms in general, there is a special controversial difficulty about hostility that makes it hard to consider it calmly. Just as discussions of sex, dependency, prestige and like motivations arouse passionate feelings in most people, so does hostility, and true detachment in dealing with it is rare indeed.

Some of this stems from prejudice and rationalization. Many people like to believe that hostility is inherited, and therefore should be dismissed as something about which nothing, for the present at least, can be done. Others believe, falsely, that hostility is a strength, that without it men and women would be left defenseless in a world all too ready to attack and exploit the weak. And some will resist the study of hostility just from the tendency of mankind to resist any new idea. The great physician William Harvey feared to make known what is now accepted as a commonplace fact—the circulation of the blood. "I not only fear injury to myself from the envy of a few, but I tremble lest I have mankind at large for my enemies, so much does wont and custom become second nature," he said. "Doctrine once sown strikes deeply at its root and respect for antiquity influences all men. Still the die is cast and my trust is in the love of truth and the candor of cultivated minds."

Besides such general reasons for shunning the problem of hostility, there are others more individual and deep-seated. Some people balk at accepting hostility as a psychological force because of hostile reactions within themselves. A friend of mine, hearing of this study, reacted quite unsympathetically. Because he was basically a man of good will, his reaction aroused my interest. He was one of those people whose hostilities were overinhibited when he was a child and as a result he felt that his wings were clipped, that he lacked the capacity of self-defense even for proper purposes. In shunning this unpleasant conflict within himself, he reacted like an ostrich, put his head in the sand and maintained that the less said about hostility the better.

Guilt for one's own known hostile reactions and deeds may also impair objective understanding, for the feeling of guilt brings conscience reactions and a need for punishment. Some people may even prefer punishment to cure and suffering to happiness. Indeed, in psychoanalytical practice it is not uncommon to see patients who truly feel that they do not deserve to be cured. This masochism, this need for suffering, is so widespread that it often extends to society in general, with a resulting feeling, usually unconscious, that mankind deserves its miseries and should not be helped toward a better life.

Freud himself started his study of the neuroses by focusing on the sexual drives and did not face squarely the vital importance of hostility until late in life, when he was unable to give it the detailed clinical attention which he gave to the libidinal impulses. However, he expanded his instinct theory into a broad dualistic view of life as fundamentally an interplay between the forces of destruction and death (Thanatos) and of creativity (Eros).

"I know that we have always had before our eyes manifestations of the destruction instinct fused with erotism, directed outwards and inwards in sadism and masochism, but I can no longer understand how we could have overlooked the universality of non-erotic aggression and destruction and could have omitted to give it its due significance in our interpretation of life," he wrote in *Civilization and Its Discontents*, published in 1931, some eight years before his death at 83.

"I can remember my own defensive attitude," he went on, "when the idea of an instinct of destruction first made its appearance in psychoanalytical literature and how long it took until I accepted it. That others should have shown the same resistance, and still show it, surprises me less. Those who love fairy tales do not like it when people speak of the innate tendencies in mankind toward aggression, destruction and, in addition, cruelty."

He discusses this further and then forthrightly declares:

"In all that follows I take up the standpoint that the tendency toward aggression is an innate, independent, instinctual disposition in man and that it constitutes the most powerful obstacle to culture."

What can we do about this "tendency toward aggression," this *hostility* (to label it more accurately)?

Each of us can focus attention upon the problem and then discern what his contribution is—and try to make it.

I believe man's hostility to man is the central problem in human affairs. I also believe it is recognizable in its various forms, that it is a disease to be cured and prevented like cancer, tuberculosis or smallpox, and that its cure will result in healthier, better living—not only for society in general but for each individual in particular.

2 *How Hostility Arises Biologically*

IF WE observe an individual member of any species—a goldfish, a mosquito, a python or a person—we see two activities predominating: the effort to survive and the effort to fulfill the life cycle. Chickens are first eggs; frogs are first tadpoles; butterflies were caterpillars. But whatever the variations, and changes in form, the basic plan is the same: first, development to maturity, then reproduction, with some care or provision for the young, then decline and death.

This cycle of life is not a remote scientific concept; it is a fundamental biological force that operates, willy-nilly, upon all of us, and any lack of surrender to it, any attempt to deviate from it or any failure to fulfill it, brings difficulty and pain.

We all know this; we meet it face to face every day in our own lives, in those of our children, in the problems of our friends and business acquaintances.

To find aid and comfort, let us look at ourselves biologically, historically and psychologically. Only in this way will we discover our true role in life, what forces impede us and how we can conquer them.

Biologically, we are, in essence, not very much. On this tiny planet of a tiny solar system, there has developed a combination of molecules in a jelly-like substance, about 85 per cent water, which the chemists call a colloidal suspension. One form of colloid we know as living matter or protoplasm. The earth's surface teems with this colloid, life, directly visible, microscopic and submicroscopic. The waters swarm with it; the sand and earth beneath our feet are filled with it. The air about us contains myriad living particles. Man is only one form of the biological life on this planet.

Why, a million years ago, did this human form of protoplasm appear on earth? Neither scientists, philosophers nor men of religion have an agreed-upon, verified answer. But we do know how it has survived—because of its adaptation to the conditions of life on this planet. The dinosaur, with its pea-sized brain and clumsy, lumbering body, did not survive; the ant, with its social organization, has existed for longer than man, probably for 50 million years. But the fact that the human race exists today does not mean that it will automatically, ipso facto, be on earth on some tomorrow. Most of us, for ourselves and our children, would not relish participation in its decay.

It is popularly believed that physical force, coupled with cunning and a dog-eat-dog attitude, is the best mechanism for survival of individuals and species. But scientific research does not bear this out. As more and more work is done on this subject it becomes clear that each form of life uses at least two major mechanisms of adaptation: the fight-flight reflex and cooperation.

According to the eminent biologist, Warder C. Allee, a leading authority in this field, cooperation not only serves animals as a protection, but also as an aid to development. His lifetime study of the simpler plants and animals reveals that the animal living in association with others increases in size, swiftness and the ability to recover from damage more quickly than his isolated brothers—the isolated animal is much more susceptible to poisons and retardation and will suffer more often from hunger and the attacks of other animals.

It is his conclusion that "no free living animal is solitary throughout his life history," and he declares that the tendency of animals to aggregate is a primitive, unconscious drive. On its higher levels, these aggregations attain refinements of organization. We are all familiar with the advanced social life of the bees and ants, with the way elephants gather in herds, fish in schools and birds in flocks.

Both leadership and "class" orders are found among animal organizations. Just as there is the queen-worker-drone order among bees, there is the somewhat despotic "peck order" among hens: each hen can peck those lower in the order than herself but must submit to pecks from those higher. Similarly, among lizards, there is a "nip order." And the same type of domination-submission order is found in other species also. Witness what a new horse goes through for several months until he finds his place in an established group. There is also a type of communication used in animal organizations. Mating calls exist in almost all forms of life from mosquitoes to birds;

bees dance in a certain way to inform their fellow hive-dwellers when and where honey can be found and birds are signaled toward migration by leader-birds.

When we turn to human societies, we find greater complexity, but a similar tendency to group, and to organize, for protection, production and communication. Like the animals, only through social living and sharing has man been able to protect himself against the elements, against animals of prey, against germs, and to find an adequate food and energy supply. But there is one difference that separates human organization from animal groupings; only among human beings have organization and aggregation been used not only for protection from other animals, but for attack on and destruction of their own kind. "One species of animal may destroy another," Allee writes in *Cooperation Among Animals*, "and individuals may kill other individuals, but *group* struggles to the death between members of the same species, such as occur in human warfare, can hardly be found among non-human animals."

Why is this so? Why are such constant features of our species as war, mass murder and hostility to one's own not indulged among the subhumans? This is probably the most important question confronting us as human beings.

The many forms of man's hostility to man are understandable as symptoms of a mechanism of adaptation run rampant.

If you are alone in raw nature, in a wilderness, your life depends largely upon the speed and effectiveness of your fight and flight reflexes. You jump or dodge or strike far faster when you take no time to think than when you do. These reactions, so essential to man's survival in cave and jungle, continue on as a sort of biological lag into our present recent living in civilizations, and may be compared to other basically normal mechanisms of the body which also overshoot themselves.

For instance, a man's body temperature rises to combat infections. It does so without thought or will on his part; it is a biological defense against disease. But it may outstrip its controls; it may go to 106°, 107°, 108° and thus kill the individual before it kills the microorganisms against which it went into action. Similarly, the membranes of the nose swell and secrete juices in order to defend themselves against irritants. But frequently they go too far in attempting to shut out dust, fumes, pollen and the like and hay fever or asthma may result.

Observing animals closely, we find certain biological changes taking place when danger threatens. Typical are the famous experiments conducted by Walter Cannon in 1928 and confirmed by others since. Cannon, working in the early days of X-ray, first mixed a little barium with a goose's food to make it opaque and then watched the stomach's reactions through a fluoroscope as the bird digested its meals under different conditions. The regular peristaltic movements of the oesophagus were grossly disturbed by threats of danger such as a barking dog. Following this experiment, Cannon tested a variety of animals, including humans. Functional abnormalities showed up repeatedly whenever the animal was under stress—and in football players before a game, in students before examinations. When threatened, the whole body's machinery goes into high gear. The blood flows from the viscera to the muscles; the heart pounds with greater force and increased speed; breathing is more rapid; the liver pours extra sugar as fuel into the blood; the whole physiology prepares for extra action.

Exploring states of fear and rage in detail, Cannon found that, faced with any threat, frustration or irritation, the animal becomes physiologically aroused for maximum effort—ready to fight or to flee. Without doubt this basic adaptive mechanism was necessary in earlier, more physically dangerous times; it is today still valuable in primitive situations where physical reflex fight or flight make the difference between life and death. But in the cooperative civilized living of today, against the moral, emotional and intellectual problems that confront most of us, this mechanism, when misunderstood and uncontrolled, is apt to be destructive of others and of the person himself, flooding his mind with hostility and fear, and creating difficulties he cannot resolve.

Before we study the varied psychological forms which this mechanism takes, let us look a little further into it physiologically. It is important to emphasize that while the two activities of fighting and fleeing appear quite different, inwardly the basic physiological preparations for them are essentially the same. The particular direction the resulting activity takes stems from the circumstances outside the animal, combined with his own inner needs, perception and judgment.

The carnivorous tiger, for instance, is aroused to *fight* when he senses the nearness of edible prey. The vegetarian rabbit, on the other hand, is aroused to *flee* when dangerous carnivores enter his territory. In the main the rabbit's flight reaction is aroused mostly for defense; the tiger's fight response for attack. Fight and flight thus represent two outcomes of a single physiological adaptive reaction. The one which prevails, in action, is largely a matter of expediency.

3 The Fight-Flight Reflex Today

WHILE NEITHER fight nor flight is effective in today's living, actual flight has become well-nigh impossible.

Until fairly recently, aroused, fearful and courageous people could put an ocean safely between themselves and oppression, intolerance and want. There were new frontiers; rich, arable land could be had for the tilling; those who wished could lose themselves among the lonely hills; and isolation from mundane problems could be sought and found in monastic orders. But today, in most parts of the world, people under stress, frustration and danger are barred by circumstances from actual flight and can only seek refuge in psychological flight.

There are four major forms of psychological flight.

1. The most harmless and often most helpful and constructive are fantasy and sublimation. These may range from hard, incessant work as an escape from emotional life through the daydreams of a tired housewife reading a movie magazine to enormously gratifying and useful creations of art and science. Fantasies, fiction, daydreams, play acting—all these provide a refuge from harsh reality, open to almost anyone. The artist knows how to handle

his fantasies creatively and can combine an element of escape with responsible productivity to make his way in the world. The normal healthy person, if he does not use his fantasies professionally, is apt to take them in small doses, as needed, and may be all the better for them.

2. *Intoxicants and drugs.* These tempt the sorely pressed with promise of quick surcease from the burdens of life. Assailed by hardships without and by emotional tensions within, many find the relief so experienced irresistible. Unfortunately, the blessing is mixed; for, as emphasized, fight and flight are basically inseparable, and in flight the element of fight is not entirely avoided. The drunkard and the drug addict seek escape in vain. Eventually destruction comes to the addict himself and to those within his sphere.

3. *"Withdrawal states"* are a third form of escape. Catatonia is an extreme example. This is a severe manifestation seen in schizophrenia. The patient is practically immobile and responds not at all to his surroundings and to other persons. If his arm, leg, head or body is placed in a certain position, he will maintain this without change for prolonged periods. This reaction is reproducible in animals, as far down the evolutionary scale as reptiles.

A less severe form of withdrawal involves the giving up of all or nearly all responsibility. This may result from quite evident outside pressures or the activating disturbance may come from within. Often the regressive back-to-childhood trend itself is very strong because of early influences on the growing child, such as overprotection or deprivation, and then only slight pressures are enough to throw it into operation. For example, a seeming pillar of the community begins to be unable to discharge his duties or pursue his regular routines. As a child, he was overprotected and, though able to make a go of life on his own thus far, has done so under inner protest and with an undercurrent of longing to return to the old responsibility-free days when he was entirely dependent upon others and had no one in home or office dependent upon him. In such a case, no very hard knocks are necessary to initiate the flight reaction, which may be expressed either in behavior alone, in loss of interest and energy for responsible activity, or with an accompanying change in mood, such as depression or apathy.

To give a more detailed example, a man with a wife and three children had fought free of the overprotection he was subjected to during childhood. He was successful in his manufacturing business and apparently stably adjusted. But he skated on thin ice. One day his partner withdrew from the business. He had depended upon this man, not only for his part in the business, but also emotionally, to an extent unsuspected by himself. The loss of the emotional support precipitated a withdrawal. He could no longer concentrate, no longer work, could not get up mornings. He witnessed the beginning of the ruin of his business and his family's security. He saw it, but was powerless to do anything by will alone to discharge his responsibilities. His mind and body simply withdrew. They refused to function. He was anxious rather than depressed in mood. He was frightened, and realistically so, by this dangerous withdrawal which to him was as impersonal as if it were a pneumonia with a raging fever. And he was as helpless before it. As noted in the author's *The Bases of Human Behavior*, such states seem related to, but not identical with, depressions and should be distinguished from them. "Withdrawal states" seems an accurate and convenient term for them.

Withdrawal also plays an obvious part in depressions and the sufferer is apt to feel that life is no longer worth while. He loses interest in people and the outside world. His physiological functions reflect this retreat by clamping down of action—including constipation, lost appetite for food and for sexual pleasure. In extreme form, depression can end in suicide, the ultimate withdrawal. But here again fight is mixed with flight. By his very act, the suicide wreaks death upon himself and takes revenge on whomever he blames for his plight. The typical depression is a crystal-clear example of flight combined with fight in the form of pent-up rage.

4. A fourth form of flight is psychological regression. It has been found that all sorts of emotional disorders, whether occasioned by inner or outer tensions or some combination of both, are in large part returns to earlier disturbed patterns of behavior which the person had in infancy or childhood. Of course, this is seen in everyone to some degree. Just as most children, when they are injured physically or in their feelings, suck their thumbs or console themselves with sweets, if they can, so many adults in trouble also turn to sweets, to food or to drink. Some frightened children seek help dependently and submissively; many adults do the same. Some even turn back to the fight reaction which served them in childhood. A man may learn more mature ways

of handling his life and dealing with other people, but if in his childhood he met every irritation with attack, adult problems may revive this pattern. (For further study of the concept of regression, the reader is referred to Freud and to Franz Alexander, who presents an especially lucid review of it in his book, *Our Age of Unreason*.)

Regression is probably an essential element in all functional psychopathology. In *phobias*, a person may fear heights or going out alone, states of feeling similar to the small child's insecurities while learning to balance on its feet or in meeting strangers. Typically, the phobic overcomes these fears when another person is with him, just as a small child's anxiety is allayed by the presence of a trusted adult or friend. "*Hysterical*" behavior, uncontrolled weeping, laughter, temper and the like are usually traceable to an early prototype. The same connection is seen in those mercurial individuals who amaze us with their shifts of mood, behaving like uninhibited children who are devastated or delighted by trifles. In *compulsion neurosis*, excessive handwashing, extreme care about dress or the necessity to count everything derives historically from training in cleanliness, manners, arithmetic and so on. An adult may express obedience through this symptom, at the same time betraying defiance against conforming by his caricature of conscientiousness and through obsessive ideas of being hostile or dirty.

Perversions also reflect regressions and returns to the sexual play or fantasies of childhood. Many *neurotic characters* and *psychopathic personalities* show quite frankly behavior in which reason and mature judgment are all too much at the mercy of the emotions, as is the case in early life when the ego, with its grasp of reality, is still relatively undeveloped. In *psychoses*, of course, the regression is deeper and involves more disorder of the ego, and even *delusions* of grandeur have much in common with make-believe. The *hallucinations* of schizophrenia become comprehensible as a return to the preverbal method of thinking in images, still utilized in our dreams.

Thus withdrawals and regressions are fundamental to the production of all the disorders which we recognize as addictions, psychoses, neuroses and infantile behavior. And this form of flight is important in *psychosomatic* conditions also, where the wish to escape is not satisfied in reality but disturbs the physiology. For example, studies of persons with peptic ulcers suggest that in some cases these can result from stress from which the sufferer cannot escape. He keeps going and the longing to escape is expressed through his stomach, which behaves as though it were hungering for food. A recent poll has supported the connection between excessive holding on to things and constipation, by the finding that persons who are especially stingy use the most laxatives. It also seems that some persons who force themselves to carry responsibilities against powerful longings to withdraw from the effort develop high blood pressure, partially for this reason.

Flight can even be a force in *criminality*, for the career criminal has relinquished the effort to make his way within accepted social limits. Here again the fact is emphasized that fight and flight are inextricably fused. One or the other may predominate, but in every case of flight observed by the author or known to him from the literature, there is also a powerful tendency to hostility, open or hidden.

In all the conditions just mentioned, through all these forms of reaction, through withdrawal, depression, manic episode, hysteria, phobia, compulsion, perversion, addiction, paranoia, schizophrenia, and the rest, and in the psychosomatic conditions in which emotions play a greater or lesser role—ulcer, hypertension, arthritis, thyroid disorders, even some allergies—however prominent the element of flight, invariably, indissolubly, the power of the fight reaction, with its rage, hate, hostility, is also unmistakable.

Psychiatry first explored and then continued to focus on flight syndromes. Freud studied and described regression in detail, but, as we have noted, only toward the end of his life did he formulate the importance of man's hostility to man. Had he lived longer, he would perhaps have developed this theme with clinical exposition, as he did the libido theory. Because of the emphasis on various forms of libidinal impulses, hostile drives have not been fully worked through clinically, theoretically or in the practical training of analysts. Thus they remain less stressed, less clarified, less understood, not yet adequately appreciated for their fateful power. Always a cause, result or concomitant of regression, hostility deserves at least parity of concern with libidinal impulses. The elucidation of hostility in its causes, effects, transformations, connections, and the means of reducing and preventing it, could well be the great contribution of this generation of students of the human mind and human motivations.

Unlike flight, actual fight is all too available to modern man and it poses a far greater threat to survival. At one end of the scale it is direct, overt and naked; at the other, indirect, hidden and even masked under the guise of justice, righteousness and love. It can be acted out, within or outside the law, by single persons on their own, by unorganized crowds or mobs, or by highly organized gangs or armies. It finds easy expression in crime, delinquency and warfare, the prevalence of which serves as an index of how widespread the problem is.

There are, for instance, in the United States nearly 2,000,000 crimes committed annually. Every hour, on the average, fifteen persons are stabbed, clubbed or shot; every hour, approximately, someone is shot. And in the past years, the crime rate has been climbing about four times as fast numerically as has our population.

We are now in an era of relative and shaky peace, but the war statistics of the recent past are germane as symptoms of the fight reaction. The wars of the generation now coming to chronological maturity have killed more than 22,000,000 and injured more than 35,000,000. And with the incredible power of present weapons, another war might well double these figures, if indeed it did not wipe out our civilization altogether. The rise in crime, if continued, could also wreak considerable havoc.

Lesser evidence of the fight reflex may be found in divorce statistics—500,000 yearly; in accidents—100,000 killed annually, 10,000,000 injured; and in 1,500,000 children annually termed delinquent by the courts.

Moreover, these statistics for the United States serve as

no more than crude guides to the overt and suggestive indicators of the hidden. One can only infer from the statistics on divorce, for instance, what hostilities were vented, directly or indirectly, in these families between the parents and toward the children and what hostilities are acted out in many other families without divorce. Nor do these figures reflect the myriad emotional problems which involve hostility in some form, directed toward the self or toward others. Few human beings are free of these.

Alcoholics, for instance, in whom the escape and the destructiveness to self and others are obvious, number 5,000,000 alone. Neurotics, who have been described colloquially as "fighting a civil war within themselves," add another 5,000,000 to 20,000,000. There are also well over a million psychotics. Of course there is some overlap in these statistics, but it is nevertheless clear that they run into the tens of millions and include a very sizable percentage of our population. In all these victims, the fight reflex and the degree of hostility varies. As will be seen in subsequent chapters, there is no functional disturbance (that is, disturbances apart from brain or other damage) without some element of hostility and usually the hostility plays an essential role.

Part Two

BASIC SOURCES
OF HOSTILITY

"From childhood's hour I have not been
As others were—I have not seen
As others saw. . . .
Then—in my childhood—in the dawn
Of a most stormy life—was drawn
From every depth of good and ill
The mystery which binds me still."

EDGAR ALLAN POE

4 *Hostility as a Disease*

WE HAVE listed some results of hostility when this biological mechanism of adaptation overshoots itself. The question which then arises is: Why does this mechanism, damaging as it is to us in our civilization, even threatening our survival, continue to exist with such force?

The answer is at once simple and complex. Certainly hostility per se is *not* inherited, or if it is, at present there is no scientific evidence whatsoever to show that hostility in humans is inherited, except as the mechanism of adaptation we have described. Nor is there evidence that any other form of neurosis is carried in the genes. Hostility cannot be passed off as something we inherit and hence can do nothing about. The fact is that hostility is a disease of the personality, transmittable from person to person and group to group, and, basically, by contact from parents to children, from generation to generation.

Indeed if the major motivating forces in each of us could develop normally, healthily, without interference or coercion from the outside, friendly social cooperation would be the result. Only when this development is disturbed during the earliest formative years of infancy and childhood, by active mismanagement or by gross neglect (whether unconscious and well-meaning or conscious and willful) does the fight-flight reaction, with its resulting hostility, flower in full strength.

In contrast to the absence of evidence for hereditary factors in determining the intensity and status of hostility in different persons, all the work on animal conditioning and the whole clinical experience of dynamic psychiatry with children and adults show the significance of conditioning influences and their basic importance in causing emotional disorders and vulnerabilities to external stresses.

(We are, of course, referring exclusively to healthy organisms and not to any effects of physical or chemical damage, deformity or impairment of the brain, glandular system or other parts of the body, nor to gross congenital developmental defects.)

This *conditionability*, this enormous plasticity and capacity for training, is one of the outstanding characteristics of the human mind.

Our minds are powered by the biological processes of our bodies, by the effects of childhood conditioning and by our adaptive reactions to external circumstance, which always evolve to some degree from emotional needs. The extent to which the various motivations are subject to influence is a result of man's very long childhood as compared with the young of other species. This slow maturing gives him vast advantages over other animals but also exposes him to greater dangers. Each person's drives and reactions are patterned by his first experiences and training, are given their main direction by the character and behavior of those who became his first models. And the earlier the conditioning, the more potent its effects and the more likely that these effects will persist unchanged for life.

Each person has a certain picture of the world, of other people, of values, of himself. It is part of the way he understands reality, part of his conscious ego. Beneath his surface conscious view, in the unconscious depths of his mind, is another picture that conforms more closely to the way he first saw things in childhood. What his senses and intellect tell him of here and now is colored, often distorted, by composite images from the dawn of his life.

When early handling of the infant and young child helps its development to emotional maturity, it increases the natural capacity of the individual for responsibility, productivity, independence (RPI)—attitudes which underlie his capacity for social cooperation. But insofar as conditioning influences impair the emotional development, form an infantile or corrupt conscience and cause disordered childhood reactions, the patterns then persist as sources of irritation, frustration and anxiety, and therefore of hostility.

To understand how this works, let us look first at the structure of the personality as we perceive it today. Our present concept is much like the old tripartite picture: that the mind is made up of reason, conscience and animal impulses.

Grouped together under the term "ego" are: (1) our powers of perception through our senses—the grasp of both outer reality and inner needs and urges; (2) our integrative powers—memory, reason and the like; and (3) our executive functions of will and control. The ego or

"I" is the conscious and most flexible part of the personality, the part which plans and coordinates action, the essence of what we call our "self," the great "organ" of adaptation to living with people. Without consciousness and its functions one is helpless, only a vegetative organism.

The term "superego" connotes those controls, models and dictates which stand over the ego. It refers to all the effects of training, all the ideals and standards adopted from the family, personal experience and neighborhood or cultural custom. It includes the conscience whose core is formed during the earliest weeks, months and years of life. The word "core" does not imply unchangeability or unalterability. Some changes in the effects of early conditioning result from the process of living; others can be brought about through psychoanalytic treatment. The nucleus of the superego is probably the innate biological tendency of the mature organism toward social cooperation as described above in animals. Added to this are the effects of those who rear the infant and young child, the main characters in the drama of its early life. Because this core of the superego is formed so early, it is usually to a large extent automatic and unconscious and therefore much more powerful and much less reasonable than one likes to think.

The animal impulses which develop out of the chemistry and physiology of our bodies are called the "id" to denote their more impersonal nature. Drives for food, sex, love, mating, dependence, parenthood, competition and the like involve the whole organism and are reflected in the mind. Our awareness of other drives fades out as they descend to lower levels of the nervous system. We are not conscious of the reflexes which maintain our muscle tone, operate our liver, or contract our pupils against bright light. Thus the psychological, what is or can become conscious, merges into the subpsychological.

It should be emphasized that mature drives, as well as infantile ones, are thoroughly part of the id. For example, mature sexual mating and parental drives are the mature id impulses and the drives toward social living are probably extensions of these. As we have pointed out, they are discernible in all animal species, with rare if any exceptions.

We are now in position to focus upon the more specific forces in the mind. As described in detail in the author's book, *Emotional Maturity*, derived from experience with patients seen over a ten-year period in psychoanalytic treatment, the major motivational forces are limited in number. The great variety of individual problems and symptoms result from different combinations of relatively few but powerful underlying major motivations.

The many thousands of material substances we know are composed of only a relatively few chemical elements. And in listing the persons treated, despite the great variety of personalities, circumstances and symptoms, the main emotional forces around which the problems revolved and from which they arose were reducible, as a first approximation, to: (1) dependence; (2) needs for love; (3) envy, inferiority feelings, competitiveness; (4) conscience and standards. In addition there were: (5)

sex, and (6) anxiety and hostility. Of a different sort were (7) sense of reality and (8) persistence of childhood patterns.

The first four appeared as basic motivations, interrelated with one another. The young child's dependence upon its parents is distinguishable from but closely connected with its needs for their love. Such dependence and receptive needs for love, if they become too strong as they are apt to in overprotected or deprived children ("momism" as it has been called by some), regularly lead to feelings of inferiority which in turn intensify envy, competitiveness, power seeking; the weakness usually causes shame and the hostility causes guilt, both guilt and shame being reactions of the superego, which includes the conscience and standards.

Where sex or anxiety is a problem this is usually secondary to disturbances in the first four motivations listed. Disturbance in the sense of reality is also a symptom rather than a force, but it is of special importance. All emotional disorders represent an excessive persistence (fixation) or reactivation of (regression to) disordered infantile emotional patterns. The disorders are "internal" or are "reactive" to stress upon *emotional vulnerabilities* which are determined by these patterns of childhood. Such patterns comprise all the motivations.

Following the grouping according to the "structure" of the personality, we would include under "id," the dependence, needs for love, envy and competition, sex and hostility. Under "superego," would come reactions of conscience and standards; and under "ego," the sense of reality.

The major sources of hostility are found in disturbances of the normal maturing of these motivations. Taking the main groups of drives, one by one, we shall now trace further how disorders of each lead to the fight-flight reaction in children and adults.

PROLONGED DEPENDENCE

Freud pointed out many times the central importance of the child's dependence upon the parents and emphasized the long dependence of the human young as the basic condition of neurotic disorders. He never developed this observation, however, as a separate paper or monograph, and its importance has not been fully appreciated. Others have studied it further, notably Alexander and Fairbairn, who sought to revise the libido theory, the better to take into account the comprehensive importance of childish dependence. There is probably always in the adult some of the child's dependence emotionally, but *how much* quantitatively is what is important. None of the infantile motivations is fully outgrown; it is always a matter of the *amount* of their influence in shaping a person's patterns of behavior.

One of the most striking facts about the development of the human personality and mind is the interplay of the *progressive* and the *regressive* forces, that is, the conflict between the *progressive* maturing from the parasitic dependence of the foetus upon the mother, to an organism capable, within limits, of caring for itself, reproducing, and caring for others, as against the tendency to *regress* from later, more mature patterns to earlier, less developed ones.

The child's drive toward independence from the parents is a basic force in the young of all species. At birth, the infant breathes for itself. It can take in food by mouth instead of being dependent on the mother's blood. With teeth it can eat other food than mother's milk. With strength and coordination, it can begin to walk and do things for itself. With curiosity, it learns the world and judgment. Then finally, at adolescence, the energies which went into its own growth begin, as full size is reached, to be channeled into sexuality, mating, reproduction, parenthood and social productivity. From being parasitic, the individual becomes parental. It is this capacity for self-reliance and for the care of others which gives the mature adult his strength, his sense of security. And only with this kind of independence comes real social maturity —interdependence.

However, there is in people also a counterforce, the tendency to be fixated at or to regress to childish dependence. The drive to maturity must conquer the pleasures of being babied. Sometimes it is the overprotection of a child which impedes his growth to self-reliance. By contrast, being forced on his own too soon can cause an aversion or recoil from it. Either way, parents who interfere with this development make an adult who, however powerful physically and intellectually, still craves a support which he never outgrew. Such cravings, of course, can rarely be gratified in life. Few adults get from mates, colleagues or friends the treatment they had or wanted to have from their parents as children. Too, the underlying needs to be dependent are usually in sharp contrast with the wish to be mature. They are apt to cause an inner sense of weakness and inadequacy which, in turn, insults the self-esteem and leads to reactions of impotent rage.

There are people who never sufficiently reach the independence or interdependence of mature adults, of self-reliant equals or near equals, which is the basis of society, and is exemplified by teamwork. This is very different from the parasitic dependence of the infant on its mother, and it is born of the maturing of this drive.

For example: A young student was so intensely hostile that he was unable to get along with his professors or classmates. He began to have ideas that everyone was against him and even broke off relations with his best girl. He became so upset that he had to leave college, but when he went to work he soon had similar troubles. It turned out that for as long as he could remember he had been pampered by his mother and older sister. His parents had been divorced and the two women had centered their interest and attention on him, praising his slightest achievement and cushioning his every hurt. Thus, when the time came to move away from home, he felt that he could not exist without them and was angered when they insisted that he try. Moreover, his retarded sense of dependence made him feel inferior to his contemporaries and enraged him through the hurt to his self-esteem. This rage at himself was forcing him into paranoia; he projected his anger onto others and felt that they were hostile and persecutory toward him. Had he not had analytic treatment, these dynamics might have taken him into open paranoia or criminality.

In others, intensified dependent needs result in broken ambitions and broken friendships, marriages and homes.

EXCESSIVE NEEDS FOR LOVE

Dependence and needs for love are closely intertwined, but are not to be considered as identical. The child's need for physical care or companionship must be distinguished from his clamorous, imperious demands for attention and coddling, just as dependence must be distinguished from such attention-getting activities as those engaged in by the man who waited until a huge crowd collected before he committed suicide from a New York skyscraper. Adults with a mature need for love fill this need successfully by giving responsible love, while persons with childish needs for love may be incapable of this and go to desperate extremes to get attention. Some of the latter will express their consuming needs for love by stressing their own abilities to be in love, fall in love, or act loving, but in action they reveal chiefly a childish demand only to receive, not give, love.

The roots of such patterns go deep into infancy. Sometimes our inherent needs for love were disturbed in childhood by being threatened, frustrated or otherwise injured; sometimes they were overindulged; sometimes the behavior necessary to get love is warped by excessive demands of the parents.

As an example of this latter, a young man was reared to get love only by being entirely submissive to a tyrannical father. He grew up with this submissiveness, but hated himself for thus thwarting his masculine independ-

Hostility as a Disease

ent drives. He went through life feeling that he must always be submissive, yet raging inwardly against it, until he came for analytic treatment and learned that he could be loved while still enjoying his independence and responsibilities. This "after-education" (Freud) or "corrective emotional experience" (Franz Alexander) can also be described as "deconditioning and reconditioning." When it occurs successfully the pathway for emotional development is reopened.

Another example was a girl with a rather brutal, negligent father who found she could win her mother's love by providing for the family in place of her father and could even please her father through his pride in her cleverness. This masculine pattern eventually clashed with her feminine yearnings for a good family life. She had to learn that, as an adult, winning love no longer was so narrowly conditioned as it was in her family, and that she did not need to be a "father" and provider but rather a mature woman.

The driving force in these people, as it is in everyone, was the need for love. All adults grow up unconsciously feeling that they can only win love if they behave as they had to behave in childhood to win it. Thus this hunger for love, which is central, forces other patterns of behavior to shape themselves to gratify it.

The need for love makes problems not only by molding these other patterns, but through abnormalities in itself of kind and degree.

Some people, though very independent in their judgments and actions, with no need to lean upon others, are yet tormented by cravings for love, so intense that they can never be satisfied. The child's needs for love are normally intense, the parents' love being its only guarantee of food, care and protection. Adults, too, require a normal ration of love. But with growth, there should be a gradual diminution in the intensity of the need to receive and an increasing enjoyment of *giving* one's share, as a marriage partner and as a parent, of what they once so clamorously demanded to *get*. Deprivation and overindulgence are two of the common errors of upbringing which disturb the normal give-get balance. If the emotional diet in childhood is too rich or too poor, then the appetite for love in later life is disordered.

Cravings for love, like hostile impulses and other needs and drives, are more or less readily displaced to other objects. In this way they often form the nucleus of an addiction. They frequently turn from the parent (or substitute) to other persons or to objects such as food or money. Hence it is not incorrect to speak of love addicts or sex addicts, or of addictions to food or money or other fantasied aims and objects for quenching the underlying insatiable, originally natural and justified childhood need. Such addictions are very difficult to correct; fortunately, however, in all analytic treatment a small shift of the give-get balance can produce a big difference, just as a very small shift of weight across the center of a balance-arm or of a see-saw can tilt the arm or board from one side to the other.

A capable young business girl had the looks and intelligence to set her well on the road to material success. Nevertheless, she was hostile and chronically depressed. At the office she made no close friends among women, but on the outside her attachments to men were intense. Repeatedly, she would fall so deeply "in love" that she would be almost unable to work; yet these affairs seemed destined to end in quarrels. As a child, she had turned to her father for affection from a mother overly occupied with social life. Busy and often unable to fill this dual role, he had substituted innumerable gifts as compensation. Now grown, this girl could neither feel comfortable with her own sex nor could her young men friends match her father's lavish attentions. Because of her excessive demands, she would lose them, and then become furious at everyone, and depressed, at times to the point of suicide.

Like exaggerated dependent needs, childish desires for love cannot be gratified in adult life. Inevitably thwarted, they form a source of constant irritation, leading to a sense of hopelessness and failure, to all sorts of neurotic symptoms, including irrational rage.

INFERIORITY FEELINGS AND COMPETITIVENESS

A third powerful source of hostility is found when desires for prestige get out of hand. In most cases, this begins with the little child's feeling of weakness in comparison with his parents. Normally, this is balanced by the assurance that, though smaller, the child is like his parents and in time will become their equal, and there is no great problem unless there is a disturbance of development. As the child passes through adolescence and reaches his full powers, he will feel secure and will find maturity with what Freud called "object interest," interest in the well-being of others for their own sakes, as enjoyable as earlier self-centered satisfactions. But if he falls short of these powers, through being so reared as to retain childish attitudes so that he feels "small," dominated, no-good or otherwise fixed in a childish sense of inferiority, a gap between himself and the adult looms large and insuperable in his mind. A continued pattern of still being a child in a world of adults persists, and he is constantly driven to prove his worth, to seek all sorts of compensation—or else to give up the struggle. This blocked development, like any other, is a fertile field for generating hostility.

Sometimes the need for prestige is directly fostered by the parents: a child may be conditioned to expect their love only when he achieves some sort of outside recognition. Much of the competitiveness between adults has its roots in the early inculcated and prolonged striving for good grades, athletic distinction or popularity. Such a basis for the giving or withholding of affection intensifies natural envy between brothers and sisters and also the rivalry inherent in a child's relations with a parent of the same or of opposite sex. Of course, a certain amount of competition is useful in growth, but when childish competitiveness is prolonged or overemphasized, it will destroy good feelings and good relations within the family and generate outside hatreds which may persist through later life.

Adults, crippled by their failure to resolve such problems, become filled with chronic hostility which shows itself in varied ways. One sacrifices his friend for a witty remark; another his country for his own position. This childish egotism can never be sated; childish envy and jealousy are never stilled. Keeping up with the Joneses,

Hostility as a Disease

beating out the other fellow—such extreme struggles for prestige have a corrupting influence on our system of values. No longer are our ideals securely those of the self-reliant frontier, the ideals of responsible men and women, producers and builders. Instead, we see the tendency to mistranslate strength and teamwork into a battle for personal status. The survival and happiness of a society depends upon how much each member contributes, not how much each member takes out.

Closely related to needs for prestige and status is the drive for power. Before his sense of reality is fully developed, the very young infant goes through what has been called "a stage of omnipotence." When the infant's needs are satisfied as soon as they arise and in an almost automatic fashion, the responsive parents appear at first as mere extensions of his wishes, cries or gestures. This response, if unduly prolonged, may condition children to the feeling that they must only want something to have willing slaves ready to satisfy them.

Power is the great assurance that one can satisfy his own needs in spite of all. Whether an adult seeks power in order to make a constructive contribution to humanity or whether he seeks it only to satisfy inner personal needs is a test of emotional security and maturity.

Power drives can take many forms—muscular prowess, sexual potency, the ability to compel obedience, sheer physical control over another. The important issue is how this power is used. When it serves the fight-flight reaction and is turned to the execution of the whole range from inconsiderateness to brutality, when it results in exploitation of any kind, hostility is evident.

The crux of the problem of both power- and prestige-demands is probably the feeling of inferiority which underlies them, a feeling which in greater or lesser degree seems to harass an amazing number of people in our civilization. Disguises for these feelings are generally unsuccessful; it takes no unusual observer to recognize that beneath most inflated egos lies insecurity.

Put generally, feelings of inferiority result from actual emotional inferiorities (usually correctible) that represent failures to develop fully to emotional maturity.

The various distorting forces that warp the mind of the infant or child for life may be subtle, hidden behind a guise of enveloping love, or they may come into the open as direct cruelty and even violence. Whatever their nature—overprotection, neglect, inconsistent training, excessive ideals, debased standards, seductiveness, exploitation and open hostility—whether stemming from misguided love or conscious sadism, the result is some form of crippling of the emotional life.

What constitutes this sense of emotional crippling is not usually conscious. Rather, the individual is apt to feel that something is wrong without quite understanding what it is. The impairment may be in any or all parts of the personality. It may be primarily a reaction of the id, for example, excessive dependence upon one or the other parent; or it may lie in a disorder of the superego, for example, in guilt, in superego harshness, in false standards, in reaching for ideals so high as to be impossible of fulfillment. Simply the lack of good loving persons with whom to identify during earliest years of childhood can also be a cause, for this may result in a poor sense of real-

Hostility as a Disease

ity, poor will power and poor control over the impulses.

Whatever the specific nature of the personality deformity, the sense of resulting inferiority is usually reacted against violently. It is an intolerable internal irritant and a threat to one's security. It is so widespread that it would be impossible to list all the ways in which different individuals react to it. We have mentioned two in discussing needs for power and for prestige. All reactions, however, have one powerful element in common: hostility.

A man feels a nameless, indefinable inferiority, which he may not even admit to himself. He cannot come to grips with its sources. He may try to change but the core of his personality is so fixed that, without treatment or unusual experiences, he is unable to do so. He is threatened but he cannot change, he cannot flee and he cannot fight the threat itself. He is blind to his inner unknown assailant. The result is what has been aptly termed "impotent rage." Irritated and threatened from within, the individual generates a constant pressure of rage and hostility that can come out in various directions—against the strong, whom he bitterly envies, or against the weak, who remind him of his own inferiority.

The following summarizes the usual route of hostility:

Influences harmful to the child's emotional development
↓
Crippling or impairment of the personality (real inferiority)
↓

Feelings of inferiority, more or less conscious
↓
Irritation, insecurity, anxiety
↓
Reactions against this; among them:
 1. overcompensatory egotism
 2. need for power
 3. rage and hostility

It is because of the high proportion of individuals filled with feelings of inferiority and with reactions to it of pride, power-seeking and hostility that we have so many of this world's problems. Few indeed are the difficulties which could not be solved with knowledge, reason and technical skill by the people getting together in a spirit of *good will*. What engenders so much of the anxiety, pain and suffering between nations, within nations, in families, in business organizations, and even in professional societies is the pride and hate which drive the men who think they know better than other men, the men who ruthlessly impose their wills with little capacity for sympathetic understanding. Yet, despite their power, these men are usually emotional cripples who have failed to achieve the ability to love. Freud has commented upon Shakespeare's Richard III, who used his physical deformity to excuse the hate and cruelty that stemmed in reality from his crippled personality. The person who shows exaggerated egotism, need for power and, above all, hostility is an *emotional* cripple—and it is of practical importance that this be recognized.

THE THREATENING CONSCIENCE AND STANDARDS

The superego, of which the conscience is a part, is largely a product of conditioning, a precipitate and clustering of training attitudes upon a nucleus of natural instinct toward social living. Most children's consciences are formed chiefly from their parents' training and attitudes, through imitation of and identification with parents. This relationship is "introjected" as the superego, and becomes a vital, powerful part of the child's—and adult's—personality. With growth it is in turn transferred or projected onto others in the form of unconscious expectations from them—expecting others to react to one as the parents did.

It does not, however, take a verbal, conscious form. Its compelling power goes far deeper than that—into the unconscious. For there is evidence to suggest that, before we learn language, our thinking is predominantly in pictures and that we return to this form of visual thinking nightly in our dreams. Apparently the young child forms images in his mind of those persons toward whom he has his first strong feelings. These images are composites, telescoping together the behavior of each of the key emotional figures, and are called "imagos." Such imagos comprise and shape the conscience and the person's pattern of attitudes and feelings toward others throughout life.

Through such techniques as free association and dream interpretation, the analyst sees how imagos shape people's views of the world. The child who has been reared with love tends to see others as loving; one who has been brutally treated behaves as though all men were his enemies. If the parents caused guilt in the child, then he will form threatening imagos as well as loving ones. And if the training was inconsistent, there are formed inconsistent, conflicting imagos which cause serious confusion in the person's mind, as a child and later as an adult.

For example, a mother filched from her husband extra allowance money for her son, who knew of this. As an adult he felt he could indulge himself even illicitly, but felt very inferior and guilty toward his father and toward other honest, hard-working men; he struggled between indulging himself illegally as his mother had done and being the responsible worker and family man his father was.

In the family is shaped the emotional pattern of outlook, feeling, reaction and behavior which will form the core of the child's personality. This conditioning begins at birth and possibly, to some extent, even before birth. The younger the organism, the more sensitive it is to emotional influences and the more easily its personality can be damaged. For example, a boy whose father had been harsh and dominating was so sensitized to this treatment that he reacted to everyone who had the least position or even air of authority with a submissive attitude which, inwardly, he could not bear and which enraged him. His father's image so ruled him that he would even become anxious in the presence of a friendly conductor on the train. As a grown man, he dreaded a trip through Europe because of having to face the authority of the customs officers. He viewed every superior with suspicion and hostility. To give in had once been too painful, too total a yielding of his will; to fight meant identification with those above him, and to his unconscious this meant that he himself would have to become the dictatorial controlling type of person he despised in his father.

Thus the formation of the unconscious images which the child will carry throughout life determines the ultimate patterns of his leadership and followership, of marriage and all his human relations. Where these images from childhood are threatening, rejecting or depriving, they form in the adult irritants which make him hostile at the least provocation.

Oddly enough, the overloving parent can create similar threatening images. Freud was concerned with the fact that the superego is often very harsh in persons who were treated, not sternly, but very lovingly during their earliest years. Persons so treated are often visited in their dreams by cruel, powerful men and beasts, and their anxiety, however directed, may not leave them by day. Freud concluded that this, too, came from repressed hostility, projected and turned against the self by guilt. When dependent, receptive wishes for love have been made too strong by being cared for not wisely but too well, the person feels these as weakness in comparison with his peers, and therefore generates impotent anger and envy. But having always been lovingly treated, he dare not confess even to himself these impulses to hate. He controls them and is in reality a kind and considerate person. Meanwhile his hate impulses are projected onto imagos which represent the incarnation of all hostility and evil. This is the devil conjured up from within and turned against himself—guilt for hostility where there should be only love.

SEX, CHILDISHLY MOTIVATED

Perhaps the best-known fact about cooperation is that it can arise as an extension of sexual-familial relations. According to Allee: "The more closely knit societies arose from some sort of simple aggregation, frequently . . . of the familial pattern." Freud, as we have noted, saw protoplasm as having two basic, innate tendencies, the one to live and come together, the other to decline and die. The tendency to come together, called "eros" by Freud, is the force leading single-celled organisms to unite and form individuals of all species which, like ourselves, consist of many billions of cells. Sex and family feeling is one expression of the underlying tendency of protoplasm to preserve and expand itself; so are the large social orders.

Sex involves and is involved in both *sensuality* and *love*. Sensuality derives from various bodily erotic zones (e.g., lips and mouth, anal region, skin, breasts) which normally contribute to and culminate in genital sensations and orgasm. Thus sex is a physiological mechanism.

But also it has a psychological content and serves to express and drain a variety of feelings. Moreover, as already noted, any strong feeling can be erotized to some degree. In the mature adult, sex is an expression of the mating impulses. In persons who have not matured sufficiently, however, sex, like other biological drives, can be misdirected and misused. Sex as (1) sensualism (visiting a prostitute in whom there is no personal interest) is distinguishable from sex as (2) romantic love (the "*grande passion*," the "great lover") and from sex as (3) part of mating (the responsible relationship involving love and stability of the home for child-rearing, and social productivity to provide for spouse and young). Of course these three forms overlap, but they are nevertheless distinguishable, and it is of great practical importance to recognize the distinctions. A man may be tempted by the sensual and think to keep all else out of his relationship to a woman—only to find romantic feelings developing and with them the arousal of the mating instinct. A fourth category may also be included: (4) the use of sex for such extraneous purposes as money making or to satisfy narcissistic needs for attention and admiration. Hence the "clinging vine," the "gold digger," the gigolo, the Delilah.

Obviously every sexual act, to be mature, need not be for the deliberate and exclusive purpose of procreation; but for maturity, sex must eventually become part of our love of others and of mating, or cause conflict. The person who continues to use sex *only* as childish play and as nothing else, who fails to fuse it with love and does not ever use it in the service of mating, making a home or rearing children does not fulfill his adult sexual role in life. The result is usually frustration and pain and guilt which cause hostility. Conversely, if overinhibited or denied all expression, sex can become a major source of anguish and anger.

There are also sources of hostility in sex feelings themselves. As the chief pathway for releasing the body's surplus energy and emotional tensions, sexuality may be used to discharge hostile impulses of varying origins.

For example, one young man had such a passion for his girl that he became more and more possessive and jealous. As time went on, he would even attempt to attack physically any other boy who made a gesture in her direction. When he came for help with his emotions, he was only a step from paranoid jealousy, delusions about his girl being unfaithful to him. He was a man who had been very deprived in childhood. His father had been cruel and his mother had merely tolerated him. Thus he grew up with intensified longings for parental love and with especial hatred toward his mother for denying him. Subsequently these feelings were transferred to the girl. Since she meant everything he had desired from a woman throughout his childhood and never received, there also lurked within him, unconsciously, impulses to revenge himself against her—and the fight-flight reaction was provoked day after day, year after year, by this conflict. Sex meant not love, but selfish demands for it and hate and attack. Only by resolving this childhood pattern could he avoid using his relationship to the opposite sex as a means of satisfying his childish needs for love and revenge. Led by his mother to see all women as beings who would surely reject him, his sex life was obstructed and, because of this, he burned with hostility which he could not understand or handle.

ANXIETY, FEAR AND HOSTILITY

In psychiatric usage, "fear" connotes an emotional reaction to a danger which is external and obviously real. For instance, it is reasonable to fear a mad dog, if one is present, or tuberculosis if one has been exposed to it. "Anxiety," however, denotes feelings of fear when no good external reason for it is perceivable, as in the vari-

Hostility as a Disease

ous phobias. Some people are so afraid of heights, for instance, that they fear going above the second floor in a city building. Generally speaking, fear is rational while anxiety is not.

However, this distinction breaks down as soon as one comes to understand the reason for the seemingly irrational, neurotic (i.e., following childhood pattern) anxiety. The man who fears heights usually does so because, looking down from them, he feels impelled to hurl himself to injury and death. Thus the danger is to him thoroughly "real"; but it is labeled "irrational" and "unreal" because it lies within the man's own motivations, in his own, apparently unreasonable, often unconscious, self-destructive impulse to jump. These "irrational" motives are only what we do not understand; when we understand them, they become entirely rational. In fact, the more we probe the reasons for neurotic anxiety, the more we find the danger is real enough and usually intelligible and rational enough, only it threatens the person from *within*, rather than from the outside world.

What is this inner danger? Let us consider a child who is in a state of fear. Studies made during the war by Anna Freud and others indicate that the healthy child does not develop excessive fear, even under protracted danger from bombings, if he has the security of his parents' presence and if the latter have maintained their own poise.

On the other hand, a child in circumstances which are quite safe physically may develop intense neurotic anxiety. Usually such a child is filled with angry impulses and usually he fears that these will come out directly or indirectly perhaps in the form of forbidden activities, and thereby bring down upon him harsh parental punishment. The dreams of children reflect clearly how they struggle with their own forbidden urges to hostile behavior and with their reactions of guilt. Usually in their nightmares, just as in the nightmares of grown-ups, the dangerous animals, witches, bogeymen and robbers are all representations, "projections," of their own destructiveness. They may also be effects of guilt and consequent tendencies to self-punishment, i.e., of hostility to self arising from the conscience or reflected back by it. Guilt stems predominantly, if not exclusively, from hostility, although this may not always be obvious at first glance. Guilt for, say, sexual transgression usually is found to be actually guilt for hurting someone through disloyalty, defiance or in some other way, with hostile wishes the commonest, most direct source of guilt and of anxiety, too.

Hostility and fear are very close in the mind. This is in part because of the unconscious mental mechanism of "projection," through which a person's own inner hostility may appear in his dreams (and in life, too) to come from outside himself, to be an outside threat which arouses his fears. This is clearly seen in delusions of persecution in paranoids, and should not be surprising in view of the fact that hostility and fear have common physiological roots in the fight-flight reaction.

This point is emphasized because it is not, as some think, simply a matter of fear causing hostility. Fear does arouse hostility—to flee or to destroy the danger. But time and again, clinically, anxieties are found to be produced *by* hostility—the *result* of it and not a cause. The reality seems to be this: Something (frustration or irritation as well as danger) makes the child angry, enraged, hostile. This hostility is against those who rear him, or brothers or sisters, or others toward whom it cannot be vented freely; it must, therefore, because of fear or guilt, love or training, or any combination of these, be held in check, controlled, repressed. It is then felt as anxiety. The pattern thus formed in childhood is then followed, in the main, for life.

THE DISTURBED SENSE OF REALITY

The adult's projections of his imagos may distort his concepts not only of individuals, but also of groups, of the social scene, of nations and of international forces. In fact, it is easier for the unconscious to emerge in relation to large and unfamiliar groups. Contact with actual people who can be seen and spoken with provides the sense of reality to correct the distortions caused by the imagos. But nations, for instance, cannot be known in this concrete way, and tend to be thought of as abstractions. Therefore, they and the leaders who determine their policies are fitted more readily into childhood symbols and imagos.

Demagogues and politicians understand this well, although they might express it in other terms. Each person has in his mind something of a "bogeyman," either the direct imago of a punishing parent or else a dream creature, formed out of his guilt and his own repressed hostile feelings. Witches and devils and other dangerous creatures of fantasy are usually projections of the person's own hostility.

There may also be a complementary figure because, let us add, imagos can be split, and often are. One patient loved his very dominating father and in part even enjoyed being under his control because this relieved him of independent decision. At the same time, his masculine pride rebelled and unconsciously he hated the subservience to his father and longed to strike out against him. He solved this conflict by always having two men in his life, one whom he could love and another whom he hated.

This so-called "splitting of the image" as a solution of the conflict between love and dependence, on the one hand, and hate, on the other, reflects the dualism of a god and a devil. It rests on the fact that it is a very difficult emotional situation for anyone to hate a person whom he also loves and on whom he is dependent. If only that person were two, he could vent both feelings. The origin and appeal of many secular and religious ideologies is that they formulate solutions for just such conflicts. Similarly, demagogues paint pictures which conform to our different imagos and, by so doing, are able to stir up infantile patterns, draw on the reservoirs of infantile hostility in the population and direct this hostility one way or another with very little regard for reality. In fact, the less reality there is to offer correction, the easier it is to manipulate the imagos and direct the hostility.

How people see nations in terms of imagos, often called stereotypes, varies greatly. To the Anglophile, the English may represent courage, determination, fair play, democracy; while the Anglophobe tends to see them as uncompromising, mercenary exploiters of their colonies. India is a symbol to some of unimaginable wealth, rare women, exotic adventure; to others it represents filth, poverty, disease, ignorance; and to still others ancient wisdom and patience.

Another aspect of domination by such imagos is people's tendency not to face the reality of "personality" in other humans (to say nothing of animals). This is partly a form of failure of identification which underlies all sorts of group prejudices. The individual members of the race or group are not seen as human beings like oneself, knowing and known by others and full of similar strivings and feelings, loving their mates and children and struggling as best they can with the universal problems. Instead, the tendency is to amalgamate the individual into a group, apply a label and see the individual and the group not realistically, but as shaped by one's own repressed feelings into a fantastic caricature, like the creations of a dream.

Labels and stereotypes like this basically represent the inner impulses and feelings of the person who applies them, usually impulses which are rejected by his "official" and conscious personality. Thus one may try to get rid of his own *feelings of inferiority* by attributing them to minority groups or to others who are in positions of lesser social or economic status such as the Semite, Negro or laborer; hating his own feelings of deprivation, he may vent this hatred on "the poor," whom he sees as representing these feelings. In similar fashion, one's own hostile impulses can be projected onto "Wall Street," unions or political candidates—just as they were onto "witches" not so long ago. Projection is a convenient, relieving mechanism, to the effect that: I am good and virtuous—

the inferiority, evil, malevolence, hostility is not in me—no, it is there, in him, or her, or it—that is where to seek it and attack it.

How the mechanism of projection operates is seen with great frankness and clarity in dreams. The night before coming for treatment, one analytic patient dreamed that he opened the door to the basement of his house, saw a big, murderous man below in the darkness and slammed the door shut in terror. A woman dreamed that she was chased through an underground tunnel by a man with a knife. Another man, also in reaction to analysis, dreamed that he was exploring underground passages when he came upon an armed intruder whom he attacked and tried to kill in self-defense. Sometimes the malign creature is not a man but a monster or a gang or the representation of some nation or other group, and sometimes the hostility appears as a force of nature, such as storm, flood or earthquake, or as a free, floating, vague terror.

Associations showed that in these dreams, the cellar and underground passages were symbols of the analysand's unconscious, the depths of his or her own mind. There the dreamers saw their own murderous impulses in the threatening figures. The figures, although formed by their own fantasies during sleep, were not recognized by the dreamers as parts of themselves, but appeared entirely alien. Hence, there was no conscious sense of *identification* with them, no empathy or sympathy, and it was therefore possible to release unbridled hostility against them.

It is this same mechanism which makes possible many

human brutalities in everyday life. A person sees as alien, feared and hated, those individuals or groups upon whom he projects his own alien, feared impulses. What he cannot face in himself, he sees while asleep in the fantasied figures of his dreams and while awake in those with whom he is not identified. Prejudice is therefore a confession. Intolerance announces something intolerable within.

Of course, fearing and wishing to destroy the stranger who is really the stranger within ourselves, the Mr. Hyde who dwells in all of us (to use Robert Stevenson's portrayal), is not the only mechanism operating in hostility to groups outside ourselves. No doubt there is a biological suspiciousness toward the unfamiliar which animals show very clearly. But the mechanism described above is, because of early repression, rather specific for human beings and central in the emotional, irrational roots of prejudice. Its fateful significance, moreover, lies in its distortion of reality to fit the emotional needs and its impairment of the adult capacity for cooperation, the foundation of human society and security.

External, "real" factors may also produce hostility, although it is doubtful whether they are ever a basic source. Even in those societies where anger and hate are encouraged as a social characteristic, early training must be given in order to insure success. For instance, in her book *Male and Female*, discussing cultural groups, anthropologist Margaret Mead contrasts the Arapesh of New Guinea with the Mundugumor. The latter are violent, hateful and cannibalistic; while among the former such hostile behavior is rare and regarded as pathological.

Dr. Mead ascribes some of the difference to the way these two groups raise their children. The Arapesh are kind to them and responsibility for all the young members of the tribe is shared by several individual families. Each child, therefore, is brought up to believe that he has many parents besides his own. If he has trouble with his real father, mother or siblings, he has a whole series of substitutes to turn to. Through this conditioning, the intense emotional relationships in the immediate family are diluted and he learns from infancy on to feel secure with many people. The Mundugumor, on the other hand, treat the child from birth in a manner guaranteed to arouse his rage. As a baby, he is pulled half-suckled from the breast, and the behavior of his parents and other adults encourages him to vent his angers freely in action.

Individual variations in hostility are also found in groups and ideologies. In groups closer home we often see how frustrations engendered by poor housing and education, by illness and poverty, tend to brutalize human beings. Clearly it is urgent to improve physical health and the standard of living throughout the world. But history has not shown that brutality and hostility are reactions to material circumstance alone. Great leaders and despots alike have come from palaces and log cabins, slums and suburbs. Semi-starvation, chronic disease or relative well-being provides only one factor in shaping personality. Probably the emotional relations to the main persons of one's earliest years, these conditioning interpersonal relations, are the great, predominant factor, all others, short of physical brain impairment, being secondary to it in importance.

Hostility as a Disease

Two levels of living must be distinguished here—the "vegetative" and the "emotional." Man must have bread and shelter in order to stay alive. But how he behaves, once these are available, is another and different matter. On the whole, there is relatively little correlation between a person's external assets and how antagonistic and dangerous he is.

There is another form of strain which may engender much hostility on a sociologic scale; it has been called by H. E. Field of New Zealand "complexity stress." It is so intense and extensive that it may influence the activity of human intellect. This is the stress so obvious in urban areas, where intellectual effort is vital to survive and to maintain standards of living. The only purpose we can consider scientifically established for any organ of our bodies is the survival and perhaps evolution of the individual and the species. Whatever other reasons may exist in reality for the human intelligence, there is no doubt that it functions in order to serve survival; in fact, it is an integrating center for coordinating what is perceived by the sense organs from without and within, and thereby effecting action to satisfy the urges of the organism.

But as urban man has become more and more removed from the direct acquisition of the necessities from the soil, from laborious muscular work and relatively simple mental processes, greater and greater demands have been made upon the intellect. The professional man and many a businessman goes through sixteen to twenty-four and more years of schooling and training. He lives in a house so complex he can no longer fully understand or keep it in repair himself. He drives a car, usually to meet train schedules. His work requires such diverse knowledge and responsibilities that he is often so fatigued by five o'clock that he needs a cocktail or a nap before he can eat his dinner. His amusements are apt to be complex, also. All he sees of the earth is apt to be in mowing the lawn or, if he can afford it, in tramping golf fairways. He expends intense intellectual effort almost constantly to get the necessaries of life for himself and his family. The political, economic, social scenes are too vast for him to comprehend despite the flood of newspapers and magazines. His own narrow sphere of activity has probably so expanded that he can no longer keep up with it fully. Symbolic is the fact that the captain of a modern ship can no longer master all phases of its operation.

It would seem as if the urban dweller, with intense, constant intellectual activity as his method of getting food and shelter, creates thereby even greater complexities by advancing technology and the increasing size and intricacy of business and other organizations, which in turn result in greater demands upon the intellect.

As a consequence, this "complexity stress," not the amount of effort alone but the number and complexity of demands, is a widespread source of emotional protest which of course stimulates the fight-flight reaction and comes to expression in many ways, from efforts at flight into sexual affairs and alcoholism to a chronic undercurrent of resentment which comes out in irritability and daily cruelties, domestic, political, occupational, and, of course, in ulcers, high blood pressure and other somatic and emotional symptoms.

Often the individual is so trapped in his position that, practically speaking, he cannot make a living without this stress. This makes it look like a source of group hostility. Yet many persons who sustain such stress to an extent which seems beyond human endurance are by no means socially hostile, dangerous or evil persons—but quite the opposite—liberal-minded, humanitarian, creative. So, although "complexity stress" is an important and widespread external, rational factor in generating hostilities, it is not critical in forming those personalities who make life dangerous for others. Basically, it is the internal factors which are the sources of hostility: external factors merely bring it out by providing pressure upon areas already made vulnerable by the emotional, interpersonal, conditioning influences of childhood.

To summarize: *Hostility is a disease of development and has its chief sources within the personality.* The distortions which cause it may be in the id (excessive demands, dependence, envy and the like), in the superego (either through hostile imagos which stimulate hostility or through deficiencies and disorders of standards and ideals), or finally in the ego (the highest faculties), insofar as an individual's whole way of thinking and outlook are warped by the persisting emotional effects of unwholesome childhood influences.

Part Three

HOSTILODYNAMIC MECHANISMS

"They went forth to battle, but they always fell;
 . . . . . .
Nobly they fought and bravely, but not well,
 . . . . . .
It was a secret music that they heard,
  A sad sweet plea for pity and for peace. . . ."

SHAEMAS O'SHEEL

5 *How We Handle Our Hostilities*

THE HISTORY of hostility begins with the history of man. As Willem Van Loon pointed out in *The Arts*, the subject of the earliest known picture drawn by prehistoric man is that of men killing one another. In the first chapter of the Bible, we find murder (because of rivalry between brothers): "And Cain talked with Abel his brother; and it came to pass when they were in the field that Cain rose up against Abel and slew him." Parallel with these acts of violence, or as Freud held, in defense against these impulses of murder, the bonds of society developed. Perhaps the first murders were the first wars—individual man against individual man. Then as morality, religion and laws developed, tribes developed —and tribal warfare. The tribes became countries, city-states, republics; the wars continued. Today nations fight nations—and there is discussion of future wars between planets. Hostility has persisted, only the ways in which it is handled show change.

It is today perhaps a hopeful sign that with the development of civilization, the moral emphasis has shifted from the feeling that wars will get you something (food, shelter, land or glory) to a feeling that wars will only help you to defend something (home, family, country and way of life). At least today excuses must be advanced for warring—not going to war frankly and exclusively for fun and gain. Is it then unreasonable to hope that if excessive hostility can be recognized as an adaptive mechanism as vestigial as the appendix, progress toward peaceful cooperation will be hastened?

The place to uproot hostility is at the source of its transmission—from within the family pattern. But to accomplish this, the virus itself must be isolated, studied and understood. The basic source of hostility lies in disorders of adjustment in childhood; but the outcome in the adult personality is determined not only by the intensity of the hostility thus created, but by the ways in which the hostility is handled.

In the technical language of psychiatry, the hostility, arising in various forms, intensities and mixtures with other motivations from the id (the biological source of impulses), is handled by the superego (the nucleus of biological-social cooperativeness plus early, and to some extent later, conditioning) and by the ego (the intellect, the conscious faculties). The ego and superego can permit or they can control and transform. To do the latter, that is, to defend an individual from unrestrained acting out of impulses, mechanisms of defense are used. (Technically these can be separated from mechanisms of conscious control, but for our purposes we need not separate them.) We pass then from the consideration of sources and characteristics of hostilities to its status relative to the rest of the personality.

The many manifestations of hostility can be reduced to seven main categories. This grouping depends mostly upon how freely the person, in his ego and his conscience, can consciously and unconsciously accept and act out his hostile impulses. Hence they can be arranged to grade from full criminality, through varying degrees and forms of repression, to transformations of the destructive hostility into socially constructive behavior. In other words, the order ranges from direct, open, hostile actions against other individuals and against society, through more or less inhibited, disguised hostility to other individuals, to actual social constructiveness. These three over-all groups may be called "antisocial," "private" (being mostly a problem to the person himself) and "social."

The seven categories fall under these three headings as follows:

Antisocial behavior, toward other individuals and society, covers:

1. The *criminal* mechanism, in which the hostility is accepted by the person, in his ego and conscience, and is deliberately acted out in antisocial form.
2. The *criminoid* mechanism, in which the hostility is not fully accepted by the person, who defends himself against acting it out directly, in antisocial form, but who is willing to act it out indirectly and within the law. This mechanism was satirized by Gilbert and Sullivan in *The Pirates of Penzance:*

"*Oh, better far to live and die, under the brave black flag I fly*

Than play a sanctimonious part, with pirate head and pirate heart."

3. The *neurotic criminal* mechanism, in which the person indulges in direct, antisocial behavior, but does not fully accept it and punishes himself for it in various ways.

Private ways of handling hostility include hostile behavior toward those close to the individual but only in personal, not in illegal or unlawful, form.

4. The mechanism of the *neurotic character* whose behavior follows a pattern in which the hostility, inadequately repressed, is not antisocial but causes suffering to the person and to those involved with him.
5. The mechanism of the *classic neurosis*, in which the hostility, repressed unsuccessfully, produces specific symptoms for the sufferer and also makes life miserable for his intimates.

The private mechanisms also include the handling of the hostility within the person without direct expression toward others, as seen in

6. The *psychosomatic mechanism*—the person who remains calm and gentle while seething inside with hostility which affects only himself by, for example, raising his blood pressure.

The *social* handling of hostility includes:

7. The mechanisms by which the hostility is *sublimated* and used constructively for the welfare of individuals and society.

How the hostility is handled, the extent to which each of these mechanisms is used in the personality, depends largely upon the maturity and health of the ego and the superego. The weaker the ego, the greater the tendency to psychotic reactions under the pressure of inner hostility.

These dynamics, as seen in clinical practice, are summarized in the chart on page 70. It shows the seven major categories on the normal and neurotic levels. The term and category "criminoid" are new but have proved their usefulness. The first four categories, from left to right, are an attempt to separate the types of persons usually lumped together under the wastebasket label of "psychopathic personality" although they may range from an innocuous eccentric to a brutal murderer.

The heading under which an individual is placed depends on how intensively and predominantly one or more of these mechanisms operates in his emotional make-up and behavior.

Such differentiations are deep-going because of the fundamental importance of hostility in all psychopathology, in all personalities, and in everyday human affairs. Hostility occupies a place in psychological processes which is quite analogous to that of heat in physical processes. All mechanical friction generates heat. All emotional friction generates hostility. Hence, just as thermodynamics is a fundamental branch of physics, so the

HOSTILODYNAMIC MECHANISMS

Form, direction and status of hostilities as seen in clinical categories. All of these dynamics probably exist in some degree and proportion in everyone, always mixed with others. They may be: (1) Latent, (2) Reactive, (3) Character traits, regular or occasional.

HOSTILITY EXPRESSED	ANTISOCIAL			PRIVATE			SOCIAL
	TOWARD OTHER INDIVIDUALS AND SOCIETY			TOWARD OTHER INDIVIDUALS BUT NOT AGAINST SOCIETY		WITHIN SELF	USED CONSTRUCTIVELY TOWARD OTHERS AND SOCIETY
	CRIMINAL	CRIMINOID	NEUROTIC CRIMINAL	NEUROTIC CHARACTER	CLASSIC NEUROSIS	PSYCHO-SOMATIC	SUBLIMATED
NEUROTIC Range, levels — Sound reality-sense, integration and control. EGO	Hostility accepted and deliberately acted out in antisocial form.	Hostility defended against in direct, antisocial form but acted out indirectly and within the law.	Hostility acted out in direct antisocial form but defenses cause self-induced suffering.	Hostility defended against and repressed is acted out in indirect, distorted form toward other individuals (but not antisocially) and with self-induced suffering.	Hostility defended against and repressed generates neurotic symptoms, indirectly affecting other individuals but not antisocial.	Hostility defended against and generally repressed produces physical symptoms, not acted out directly or indirectly against other individuals or society.	Hostility direct or transformed is used for welfare of others and society.
PSYCHOTIC Range, levels — Marked distortion by emotional forces of reality-sense, integration and control.	PSYCHOTIC EQUIVALENTS						

More toward others, antisocial ←→ Hostility Directed ←→ Less toward others, more social
Less mature, social, effective ←→ Superego ←→ More mature, social, effective
Accepts hostile impulses, behavior ←→ Ego ←→ Rejects hostile impulses, behavior

How We Handle Our Hostilities

dynamics of hostility is a fundamental branch of psychiatry and can properly be called "hostilodynamics."

Of course, no one individual handles all of his hostilities exclusively in the manner described for each category. These sound like sharp divisions, whereas, in reality, people not only show mixtures of these mechanisms, but if a large series of actual cases were arranged in order, they would form a continuous spectrum, a gradation from one extreme to the other. Nevertheless, just as separate colors can be perceived as such in the solar spectrum, as in the rainbow, even though the whole is a continuity, so these seven major categories can be differentiated by the prominence of one or another mechanism for handling the hostility.

A further distinction in real life involves the extent to which motivation is "internal" or "reactive." A quite social person, by no means given to criminal acts, can generate such rage under certain external conditions that he loses control of himself, by-passes his judgment and standards and commits acts which are "out of character." Under sufficient external pressure, especially if it bears on his particular emotional vulnerabilities, the most stable individual can break down (or break out) into hostile behavior. On the other hand, many persons in quite satisfactory life circumstances indulge in cruel behavior out of internal motivations. Thus in every category, the hostility and the way it is handled, i.e., the hostilodynamic mechanism, may appear as:

(1) Latent
(2) Reactive to unusual stress

(3) A character trait, showing
    occasionally
    regularly

Another feature is of great importance. External or emotional pressures can alter the intensity of an individual's hostility and the way in which he handles it. Therefore it is possible for a person to shift, temporarily at least, from one category to another. But how easily the latent hostility can be aroused in him and how far he will go depends chiefly upon his *basic character patterns*. Under the influence of physical or emotional hardships or under the sway of demagoguery, there is an increasing chance that the conscience may be lulled or bribed, or that the grasp of reality may weaken and hostility break through or neuroses or psychoses may develop.

Our chief concern will not be with these mechanisms as evoked by traumatic external events and acted out in brief, transient episodes. Rather our attention will be directed to persons who show them as part of an accustomed way of life, as a permanent character trait.

The distinction between "private" and "antisocial" hostility reflects a contrast which is obvious in life. Many people treat their own families very differently from other individuals, other groups and society at large. A man may be a criminal killer and involved in all sorts of illegalities, and still be kind to his wife and children. Conversely, another may be a constructive figure in his occupation and in the community and yet be a tyrant on the domestic scene. You may spend a delightful evening with the charming John Does but have little idea of what happens once they shut the door behind you.

As we have repeatedly stressed, hostility is a result of disordered and persisting infantile impulses. How a person handles these depends not only upon their form and intensity, but upon his over-all maturity and upon the structure and strength of his ego and superego, which are also determined preponderantly by his early conditioning.

On the psychotic level, for instance, the tendency to regress to childhood patterns is strong enough grossly to derange the perceptive, integrative and executive functions of the ego. Insofar as psychosis is only an extreme of neurosis, it reveals no basically new mechanisms for the handling of hostility. The fundamental feature is the relative weakness of the ego in coping with motivations from id and superego, so that the person's feelings can distort his ego functioning, including his thinking and sense of reality, and even lead to frank delusions (as of persecution or any other kind) and hallucinations. Extremely psychotic persons are, just because of this, usually easily recognized. However, in the milder cases the person may exercise considerable influence in society without being discounted or even recognized as psychotic. Many an individual distorts only that portion of reality which serves the purpose of his hostility. Plausible in most areas, he may even become a fringe political leader and, by his very extremism and intensity, cause an emotional resonance in others, expressing in magnified form personality tendencies which are latent in his followers.

An historic example of this, as one reads history, was Aaron Burr in his relationship with Jefferson. Even though Burr himself induced his own disgrace, he generated hatred for those whom he held responsible and then apparently became quite unrealistic about them, including Jefferson in particular, in order to justify his hate. In effect, he said not "I hate him because he offended me," but "I hate him because he is an enemy of mankind." Through this he took in many Jefferson-haters. The disturbance in the sense of reality of such people may be only partial and only in that one sphere in which the hostility requires it, but this may make the person more rather than less dangerous in public life.

The same hate, rage and impulse to attack may come out in the criminal in direct murder, in the depressed patient in overwhelming self-reproach or even suicide, and psychosomatically it may find expression in an epileptic attack or some other illness.

It may even show up disguised as pleasure. This exercise of a function for pleasure rather than in use for survival is called "erotization." Franz Alexander, in his *Fundamentals of Psychoanalysis*, sees it as an expression of surplus energy not needed by the organism for growth, propagation or maintaining a livelihood. Muscular powers are used for enjoyment in sport. People eat because they like it as well as for calories. Similarly, some people fight, or create fights, because they enjoy them.

This is seen in varying degrees throughout history. In the Roman circuses, condemned men and women were turned loose among wild beasts to be torn to pieces for the pleasure of the audience. Among some tribes of

How We Handle Our Hostilities

American Indians, fighting was frankly a form of play. Even today, war is not wholly a means to an end. Little children play war for fun; adults enjoy prize fights, wrestling matches, dramas of violence.

In sadism, some individuals gain their chief pleasure out of torturing others. There are people who only reach sexual orgasm through inflicting pain on another in lesser or greater degree. Here there is actual sexualization of the hostility. As Gregory Zilboorg noted in his *Psychology of Criminal Acts*, some murderers experience multiple orgasms during the deed. So did some soldiers when shooting an enemy or when in extreme danger. Obviously certain persons get their sexual satisfaction out of being threatened, beaten or otherwise badly treated. In sexual masochism, the need to be punished is erotized and becomes an essential component of gratification.

As we have noticed, there is a tendency for any strong emotion to be connected with sexual feelings, i.e., erotized. All during life, every person has sex hormones circulating in his blood stream and, especially during maturity, is under constant sexual pressure. This pressure is reflected subjectively in the mind which it fills with sexual impulses and fantasies, more or less repressed, disguised or elaborated. A prime function of the mind is integration. It naturally integrates the sex drives and feelings with other motivating forces. Because of this pervasiveness of the sexual feelings, hostility can become mixed with them so that hostile aggression is part of the sex drive, and so that sexual feelings accompany hostile aggression. Within limits some hostility admixed with sex (in the male, for instance, in the expression of mastery) is usual and normal. But where actual injury is practiced for sexual pleasure, this is sadism. And where, through guilt or other reactions, hostility is directed toward the self and this is mixed with sexual feeling, sexual masochism may result, though a small amount is probably a normal part of female submissiveness.

Thus, the status of hostility varies according to (a) the early conditioning which by stimulating hostility determines its intensity in the id; (b) the proportional strengths of the disordered infantile patterns and the mature motivations; (c) the different forces which keep it going, such as frustrated infantile demands for love or prestige; (d) the direction and degree of fixation of the hostility on certain imagos and its transferability to other persons; (e) the degree to which it is accepted in its different forms and directions by the superego; (f) whether the superego operates in advance or with constant effectiveness or whether it permits acting out and then brings down punishment; and (g) the extent to which the conscious ego accepts the restrictions of the superego or to which it feels justified in accepting the hostility with or without later punishment. All this will be made concrete and easily comprehensible by the following discussion and examples of each of the categories.

THE CRIMINAL

Our goal is now to clarify and emphasize the major dynamics that distinguish each category. We shall be speaking of dynamic mechanisms, of ways of handling hostility which probably exist to some degree in everyone and which may reveal themselves in response to external as well as internal pressures. Bearing this in mind, let us focus upon the type of case in which such patterns are internally motivated and are an essential part of the individual's personality.

The literature devoted to the genetic-dynamic sources of criminality is relatively meager, though now rapidly expanding. The older theories that criminality is congenital and hereditary can be given little credence. The facts to establish such theories are totally inadequate. And while it is certainly conceivable that physical, developmental defects in the brain itself may result in uncontrolled criminal behavior, these cases are not the ones which concern us and any theory as to congenital or hereditary factors producing such functional effects in the intact organism still carries the burden of proving itself.

We are safe, then, in assuming that, according to present knowledge, the child who develops into a criminal character either has been subjected to gross mistreatment during his early years or a model for this kind of behavior has been provided by one or both parents or by others to whom he was emotionally attached. Without this background, even strong influences toward criminality fail.

For instance, in "crime areas" the accepted social standard among a child's playmates frequently involves direct juvenile gangsterism. If a child does not accept this neighborhood ideology and join in with the gang, he not only may be ostracized and despised, but his actual physical safety may be threatened. Nevertheless, not every child in such a crime area becomes a delinquent. If the family influence has been stable and healthy enough, despite all group pressures and threats of retaliation, he will not accept criminal patterns of behavior. So, too, in later life, a man or woman under great external pressure and example may, in spite of every temptation, never behave in a criminal fashion because this is too foreign to his personality. The twig must have been bent in childhood in the direction of crime for the tree to be so inclined.

We call "criminal" the *kind* of person whose make-up is such that he accepts, as part of his accustomed behavior, his hostile feelings against other human beings and is willing deliberately to act out these feelings. He may injure other people through crimes against their property, such as theft, or through crimes against their person, such as assault. An extreme example is the professional killer who is available for hire or the racketeer who hires others to commit acts of violence.

The so-called normal or successful career criminal may show no impairment in sense of reality or intelligence, nor will the restraints of conscience and social feeling seriously hamper his overt hostile behavior.

Criminality is also seen in different form among individuals who commit crimes more for emotional satisfaction than for gain and economic security.

As for what crime is, throughout our discussion, we treat crime in the biological sense of injury to life and the living, particularly human life and human living. By injury, we mean not only bodily damage, mild or murderous, but anything which impairs development and adjustment, individual liberty and happiness. An injury is thus considered criminal if widespread perpetration of it would threaten the foundations and functions of society.

Let it be noted that our definition is basically independent of any laws which may or may not exist in a particular community. In fact, if the laws injure human life and living, then the laws themselves may be termed criminal. This would hold true in our mind even for a savage community like the Mundugumor, mentioned previously, wherein the mores are described as involving free acceptance of a relatively large amount of hostility in violent behavior and the noncriminal citizen is the exception and the eccentric.

Of course, the quantitative factor is of great importance here. Not every inconvenience which someone imposes upon us need be called a crime; essentially we are seeking for the *quality* which can be isolated and properly described as criminal. This quality seems to be an inner, psychological one, a mechanism which conceivably can and perhaps does exist in *quantitatively* different degrees in everyone. *Its essence is an individual's acceptance in his ego of sufficient hostility for him to act it out with relative freedom against other human beings for selfish personal purposes.*

An analogy with illness may clarify the use of the term "quality." If a person has a sniffle, he is not considered by himself or others to be sick. If he has a tiny splinter in his finger, he does not call it an injury. But while these are mild, perhaps even negligible conditions, still their essential quality is harm to the organism. So one would not label a minor offense against a person or his property, such as maliciously slighting his name or trampling his lawn, a crime. Nevertheless, such an act, however negligible in quantity, may in its quality be criminal.

This formula naturally must be used with caution. Human behavior is difficult to judge. Usually it is essential to know the motives. Suppose a person injures, even kills, another for purposes of self-defense. If the main motivation is mature, and life-preservative for himself, his family or country, if the act is not done out of egoistic malevolence, then it lacks the essential quality of criminality. The purpose of an act may even be constructive and pro-life though the means used may be in a hostile form. For instance, the policeman who kills a killer solely to defend society and its members is not acting criminally; but on the other hand, if he commits the same act out of personal motives, such as thrill, revenge or for personal gain, then psychologically the act itself is criminal despite its socially good results. Because of the immaturity of the world in which we live, peace must often be maintained through force, and, unfortunately, only too frequently men use the authority of law as a mask for their own criminal mechanisms.

Thus to understand the hostilodynamic mechanism in a given person and circumstance, not only the act itself must be considered, but its external purpose in the mind of the doer as well as his internal feelings in the doing of it. This distinction is seen repeatedly in fiction. The hero presumably kills "more in sorrow than in anger," and only out of the feeling that it is for some worthy, necessary purpose, to protect the heroine or to defend his country or to achieve peace. The villain, however, enjoys his evil doings and freely accepts cruelty as a means to most selfish ends and often even as a satisfaction in itself. The distinction may seem less sharp when the rationalization used to explain cruelty is revenge, for revenge is usually infantile and criminal, a fight-flight response, and profound truth and insight into maturity and society is expressed in the Biblical words: Vengeance is mine, saith the Lord.

Happily for human welfare, the majority of people do not find such hostile impulses acceptable to their consciences or their conscious judgment. *Society rests on the capacity to control and sublimate hostility*. Everyone has been in situations where, impelled by anger, he has nevertheless not felt free to satisfy his hostile impulse and has restrained it. This is "suppression" or conscious control, exerted by the ego. Many of us, too, have been trained from infancy to restrain or even reject such impulses entirely. These then become "unthinkable" and are checked before they can reach consciousness. Such automatic, unconscious "repression" is powered by the superego rather than by the ego as the conscious control. Impulses thus blocked from direct expression may seek other paths and may produce neurotic, psychotic or psychosomatic symptoms instead of criminal behavior. More about these later. We shall now sketch a criminal case history.

It would be superfluous to present as an example of the criminal mechanism a man who is accepted and known as a criminal. Such examples are all too available for the reader to see in life, in the press and as dramatized by writers. For this reason we have chosen to discuss a person in whom one would not expect this mechanism to be prominent, but one who was a killer *psychologically*.

He was a married business executive, smooth and charming in appearance and manner, and very successful in public life. Privately, however, he was coldly hostile to his wife while at the same time professing to be madly in love and full of admiration for her. In his office he was calm in exterior; at home he was tossed on a seething sea of emotion, and more than once he had deliberately destroyed expensive possessions which his wife valued. Now, when he came for treatment, he was thinking of killing her.

The background for his distortion of personality was traceable, as always, to specific warping influences during childhood. His father had been much preoccupied with his own affairs and remote emotionally from the mother and children except for one daughter toward whom he showed great favoritism. His mother was an unstable woman of violent temper and hates. She was free with family beatings and on one occasion inflicted rather serious injury upon one of the children of the neighborhood. It is not known whether or not she fought with the father physically, for when the man we are discussing was not yet six, his mother left home and children. The father remarried soon thereafter; his second marriage was also of short duration.

Our man was not conscious of any hostility against his father or his petted younger sister. All of his conscious hostility was turned against the image of his mother, though he had no concrete conscious memory of her and he could not recall what she looked like, how she acted or dressed or even any incident about her. What remained in his mind was the picture (imago) of a person whom he blamed for all the unhappiness and frustration of his childhood. Whether or not the father directly encouraged this, the imago of his mother became the object of his every resentment. He grew up with very few friends, continuing toward other persons the emotional remoteness which he experienced from his father and which he took over as a defense.

The only person with whom he had any sort of warm, emotional relationship was his younger sister, whom he both loved and envied. No one can develop properly nor can most people even live without at least one reasonably good human relationship. In all probability, this affection for his sister saved him from severe mental disorder. It became the model for what friendly rapport he was to be capable of. Later patterns of kindliness which it contained repeated themselves toward his children and served to protect them from his otherwise inexorable hostilities.

What in his wife's emotional make-up led her to marry him need not concern us here beyond her appreciation of his fine qualities plus identification with him and a masochistic attraction to danger which grew out of her own childhood. His feelings toward her repeated at first the profound longing for a good mother which he had felt during the earliest years of his life, but of course, as an adult, this longing was far too primitive and infantile. It was not the need to love and be loved which is appropriate in maturity but contained all the intensity of the small child's demands. As such, it was foredoomed to frustration. Thwarted in this need, he soon felt toward his wife the same disappointment he had felt as a child toward his mother—and a similar criminal implacable rage. And his mother, with her beatings, provided the model for venting hostility in actual physical violence.

Meanwhile, a neurotic mechanism of hostility also showed in overanxiety about his children. On rare occasions he might lose control and strike one, but then would soon feel guilt and remorse. Though jealous or resentful of them at times, following the pattern toward his younger sister, he could not, without inner conflict, take out his hostilities upon them. He repressed these feelings, but under their pressure he developed a sense of anxiety about the children. Neurotically, he felt that they were in danger, without realizing that the danger lay in his own motivations, and he was overly protective toward them. (Periodically, new reports tell of a stable, churchgoing parent who one day kills spouse and children.)

By contrast, the hostility toward his wife became conscious. Clearly the ego and superego permitted this because of self-justification. Having unconsciously placed his wife in the role of his mother, he now felt free to revenge himself upon her for his mother's beatings and the desertion of him as a child. He planned her murder precisely and repeatedly, never aware that this was following his pattern of feelings toward his mother in childhood. This acceptance of hostility and the willingness to act upon it is unmistakably the criminal mechanism; it convicts him psychologically, and although his wife died a natural death, and he never carried out his designs against her, this man was psychologically, in his intent, a criminal.

One added word about this case. This man's infantile impulses did not discriminate between his mother and his wife. This failure is probably much more common in criminals than is generally believed and explains those superficially bewildering incidents that appear from time to time in the newspapers. A vivid example of this was the recent case of two men in their early twenties who assaulted and beat to death a harmless, middle-aged man whom they had never before seen and who was not worth robbing. Clearly whatever or whoever had shaped and generated their hate and hostility during their formative years, it was such that now it could be taken out on almost anyone, even on a complete stranger. This displacement is a basic characteristic of hostility; there is a spread to other persons, animals or even inanimate objects of the child's revengeful hatred of his original offenders.

THE CRIMINOID

Ugly and anti-human as is the frank criminal, there is another type of personality which can be equally, if not more, sinister. This type complements the criminal, makes organized crime possible and is widespread enough numerically to be considered a characteristic of our times. We have termed him a "criminoid." While he is a person who stays within the letter of the law, his way of living, his decisions, his political attitudes reflect his hostility to mankind and his subtle destructiveness to society and its cooperative goals.

The overt criminal is relatively direct and honest about his antisocial hostility. As Alex Comfort pointed out, he even serves a sort of constructive function for society in providing an object for the hostilities which constantly simmer among us and seek expression in many ways.

However, the type of individual to whom we now call attention does nothing openly for which he could be called into court as a criminal. His hostility, although acted out, is masked and disguised as legal and proper. Indeed, he may appear to himself and to a great part of the community as a model citizen, "a most honorable man." What we are describing by the term "criminoid" is again a psychodynamic mechanism, a way of dealing with hostile impulses. But this mechanism does not allow these impulses to be acted out directly as in the criminal dynamic. Rather, they are acted out indirectly, usually impersonally and within the law. This mechanism, like all the others, may play a minimum role in a personality or be of such proportional strength as to dominate it. It, too, may be latent, reactive to unusual stress, transient, occasional or a permanent character trait.

At one end of the criminoid range is behavior which is so close to the directly criminal that it is transitional between these two types. This would be exemplified by the man whose inner restraints and defenses are such that he cannot himself kill anyone but can arrange for another to commit such an act. At the opposite extreme are minor manipulations which are within the law, injure no single

How We Handle Our Hostilities

person directly and are often valued as being "smart." The "dual conscience" of some businessmen has frequently been described—he who would never personally harm the poor widow and her children but as a business matter will foreclose their mortgage to his own profit. Similarly, several decades ago, it was not uncommon economic practice to exploit immigrant workers through forcing them to rent jerry-built company houses and to buy goods, often inferior, priced and sold by company stores. Labor unions also have tolerated forms of blackmail and racketeering.

Overt criminality is generally all too evident as such; neurotic behavior, too, is attracting increased recognition. But criminoid behavior, masked and camouflaged as it is, eludes notice and has not been defined and brought into focus.

Possibly this is because the criminoid mechanism permeates so many of our attitudes. We tend to avoid thinking of accepted activity in moral terms. "Oh, that is just commonplace—politics or business or labor or human nature is like that," we say. In the statistical sense of average, criminoid behavior may even be "normal." But just because it is "normal" in India to get smallpox or in America to get dental caries, these conditions are no less of a disease or a problem—they are not normal in the sense of healthy. In fact, the acceptance of the criminoid as normal makes him even more of a serious threat to our society.

Let us now look at who some criminoids are. In politics there are the demagogues and hate-mongers, those leaders and groups who seek gain at the expense of others. In present-day America, there often seems to be an affinity between politics and criminoid activity. Certainly, all of us know many men and women who, though apparently personally stable themselves, back demagogues who incite to acts of violence and hatred. All of us also know of public officials who use the cloak of authority to protect crime rings, "deals" and bribes. We also know that certain pressure groups may for their own gain favor inflation or depression or even war.

Such behavior may be "normal" in the sense of "average" in the political and economic life of society. But our measuring rod is not statistical, but psychobiological. It is a scale of emotional maturity, derived from observing the contrast between the egocentric, hostility-prone attitudes of the infant and the outgoing givingness of the good adult, not only in humans but in other animal forms.

Criminoid mechanisms may be prominent in the lives of many persons without being recognized consciously by the people involved. Few people aid criminoids with a view to doing harm deliberately and maliciously; most simply do not know any better, and some even think of themselves as very virtuous or smart.

To illustrate how this operates on a different level: A young man of high caliber and quite mature in his capacity for love and sympathy, who would not knowingly hurt anyone in any way, had strong feelings of inferiority, the result of overprotection by his mother during childhood. Insecure in his masculinity, he believed in sincere good faith that a young man of any virility should prove himself by "getting women." Being attractive and highly sexed, he seduced, lived with, and finally abandoned many girls, causing some of them serious unhappiness. Yet to him it was only doing what he thought was expected of a "real man," and when he learned the nature of maturity and saw what he had been doing, he was able to find less criminoid, more adult modes of expressing his masculinity.

In politics and in business one sees many a person who accepts democracy and freedom as permission to grab from and outwit other persons, maintaining that they are doing the admirable thing in achieving "success" for themselves in their field, despite the cost to others, just as the young man mentioned above achieved his success by using women.

Not that success is undesirable. But it is not a purely egocentric matter. True success is measured by constructiveness, by contributing to the well-being and happiness of others: one's family, friends and society—and humanity. Beethoven, Jefferson, Lincoln, Newton, Einstein, Harry Lauder, Jim Thorpe, Luther Burbank, Freud. True success in any field is measured by the excellence of the person's responsible contribution, what he has given to others, be it for their safety or their entertainment or for the advance of the human spirit. The tiny infant is egocentric, even parasitic, for its task is its own development; but society, and all it means to the infant and to all ages, is our means of security against nature. Our health, pleasure and advance are only made possible by society through the contributions to it of each adult. When an individual's self-love is primary and too strong, it is very apt to lead him into harming, not helping, others—and himself—into criminoid behavior, however righteous he may seem to himself in his own "self-image." Through his impatience for personal success, he is apt to sacrifice the very rewards for which he burns himself out. More hostility is then aroused and this hostility (as does all hostility), in turn, wants some person or group to hate—a scapegoat. Demagogues rise to power by offering objects for this hate. Rationalizations are readily found. And thus the criminoid mechanism becomes widespread.

Not all criminoids are important leaders. For example, let us look at the case of a small-town woman, raised in a modest, middle-class family. At eighteen, attractive and with a superior intelligence, she married the town "catch," the only son of a well-to-do real-estate broker. The young man, unlike his father and wife, was not a go-getter. His chief ambition was to write a history of the area in which they lived and he preferred poring over the early settlers' records to buying and selling property for his contemporaries.

At first his wife was content with her marriage. The business continued to thrive under her father-in-law's direction and the income from it and her position in the town satisfied her needs to be "first" and favored.

Then, however, the Depression came, the father-in-law died and the business was in danger. The husband forsook his career as a historian and devoted himself unflaggingly to the business in an effort not only to maintain financial security for his family, but even beyond this to satisfy his wife's needs for social prestige. It was an uphill fight. Increasingly frustrated by lack of money and success, the wife began to taunt and blame her husband to his friends behind his back, meanwhile showing him a contempt and coldness which gradually undermined his stamina and his self-respect. He began to drink and neglect the children, for his mounting repressed rage at his wife made him anxious and depressed. As these tensions in the home increased, he drank more and more heavily, and in desperation attempted suicide. Now his wife rejected him totally. His reputation was ruined. He had no one to turn to. He was not sufficiently mature to handle matters. Soon afterwards, he developed mild schizophrenic symptoms, and the situation became such that he had to be committed to a state hospital.

His wife, far from standing by him when he needed her and when she could have saved him and kept a father for her children, was glad to be rid of him and to be free to pursue her ambitions unhampered. As times improved, she advanced in a store where she had found a position, and after some years became assistant to the manager. The children had a difficult time, for the relief of the tension between their parents was bought at the price of losing their father, who was their chief emotional support, and thereby their only model for good human relationships. The mother herself was callously indifferent to them. She entrusted their care to what hired help she could find and, when this failed, she would often lock them in separate rooms, tying the youngest to a chair to keep him out of mischief. Both children developed nightmares and a variety of behavior problems which signified the inevitable arousal of hostility and hate and the warping of their development.

Her relationship to society was similar in feeling. Though desirous of respect in the community and very charming in her surface business and social relations, she inwardly despised all those who were beneath her socially. True to type, she fawned upon those whom she saw as stepping stones. Where she worked, she tacitly encouraged certain sweatshop practices, and in the community she strove to keep minority groups off all local committees. After a few cocktails, she might reveal that she believed that they should be exterminated. She also drove her car in such a manner that it was an actual danger to others.

On the whole, however, this woman's behavior would not be considered antisocial or criminal. She could quite righteously justify her actions. The hostility behind them was, for the most part, indirect. The fact that it helped to ruin the lives of her husband and her children was considered only a family matter. Her civic attitudes were considered her own business. Her behavior was not in any way illegal nor could anyone step in to check her without being accused of meddling in purely private affairs.

But the *criminoid* nature of this woman is obvious and the lack of neurosis (in the narrower sense of the specific symptoms) probably shows best in the fact that she could not only behave the way she did but could do so without accumulating any really effective feelings of guilt. If she had had more of a conscience, she could not have acted out her hostilities to such an extent, even in this indirect form. Very often one sees people do similar things, meanwhile piling up so much guilt that it forces them into some type of emotional or psychosomatic disturbance. Such cases, wherein the hostility is more checked toward others and channeled more toward the self, would move to the right on our chart, that is, toward the neurosis category. But this woman was able to go her hostile way without adequate internal checks upon her hostility, acting it out toward both intimates and social groups and thus becoming a truly criminoid character.

Other families broke up during the Depression for similar reasons; other women have been forced to work under conditions less than optimum for their children. Too, the kinds of prejudices which this woman held are not unusual in a small town where class lines are rigid. But this woman did not merely reflect the attitudes of a family or group situation; nor did all members of her group accept such attitudes nor behave as she did.

Criminoid groups are analogous to "crime areas." We have already noted that a certain percentage of boys in crime areas do not go along with the gangs. This woman's social group might have provided the temptation, opportunity and encouragement for some of the behavior in which she indulged. But there must have been something in her own motivations which led her to the particular patterns with which she handled her hostilities. In brief outline, these inner motivations and the early influences which shaped them were as follows:

Her mother had also been a beautiful girl, without education but deeply ambitious to "amount to something." Disappointed in her marriage to a shiftless man, she had not wanted children but she was determined that this child should realize all the goals she herself had not achieved. Increasingly neglected by her husband, she drilled her daughter in dress and deportment, and took domestic jobs so that her child might have voice and piano lessons. But she did not give her the two great essentials: unselfish love and respect for the child's own personality. And the father also resented the child as a person.

As the child was shaped, so the woman became. Following the pattern of her own and her mother's reactions to the father, she felt only contempt for men, and her fine social manners covered the hatred and rebellion she felt against the depriving, dominating mother who had imposed these manners upon her.

It is a general fact that an adult behaves toward others in later life according to two chief responses to his parents or their substitutes. (1) He identifies with the parent and acts as the parent did during the person's childhood; or (2) he reacts toward other people with the same feelings he had toward his parents as objects. Usually, probably always, there is some mixture of these two: identification with, and object relation to, the parent.

Our woman, identifying with her mother, tended to treat her husband and children as her mother had treated her father and herself. She turned from her husband when he failed to live up to her expectations; and she neglected her children (as her mother had neglected her) for the pursuit of the goals her mother had instilled within her. But also she harbored feelings of revenge against her parents, and, in retaliation, lived out toward her husband the hate and rejection she had felt toward her father and mother. Her capacity to love, to feel good will toward others, was crippled by this lifelong, repressed resentment for the lack of love and understanding during her childhood and for the disregard of her own personality under the imposition of her mother's ambitions. Beneath her surface conformity burned pathological, constant and intense hostility.

Why did these hostilities not come out more openly? Because there had not been the model for naked violence in her upbringing to enable her to indulge in this directly herself. Instead, the pent-up feelings were forced into other byways, perhaps no less harmful, but not as overt. Viruses are such tiny organisms that they cannot be seen under the usual microscope, as bacteria can. Yet the viruses can produce in our bodies just as serious diseases as the relatively large bacteria. Indeed, just because they are so small, they elude direct study and hence are today the more dangerous enemy of man. Like these viruses, the hostility which finds expression in criminoid form through masked interpersonal and group cruelties may achieve ends just as destructive as frank criminality, which, like bacteria, is open for all to see.

THE NEUROTIC CRIMINAL

As we have pointed out before, the differences among the seven categories are based not only upon the form and intensity of the hostility and its mixture with other motivations, but also on how the hostility is handled by the ego and superego. In the neurotic criminal, hostile, antisocial impulses break through into behavior, but they do so only against strong opposition from the individual's judgment, training and conscience. These ego and superego influences operate in various ways, two of which deserve special mention here.

In one type of case, the inner opposition from the superego is quite thoroughly repressed and is not conscious. On the contrary, one's ego consciously accepts the antisocial impulses and he appears to himself and to others as an unalloyed criminal character. Ostensibly, he approves of this in himself and in his acts; but meanwhile his conscience, though it operates without his awareness, grows more and more powerful, grinding away silently but no less effectively. This is the sort of criminal who repeatedly gets caught or otherwise manages to bring suffering on himself; someone who—like Lady Macbeth—can freely plan and initiate murder, apparently with the most complete determination and no conflict at all, but, after the deed, finds himself shaken with guilt and brings about his own punishment.

In a second type, the superego forces are much more conscious, although, like the unwilling alcohol addict, not enough to alter or control the patterns of the individual's behavior. His ego judges it harshly; he knows that it does not conform to his own or society's standards and may even seek psychiatric treatment in an effort to change. But meanwhile, his need for punishment is great. Because the former, Lady Macbeth, type is so well known to us we will present an example only of this second kind of neurotic criminal.

He was an accountant in his early thirties who came for psychoanalytic help after serving a term for embezzlement. He was a family man with a wife and two children,

How We Handle Our Hostilities

a kindly husband and father who enjoyed his home to the full.

With high intelligence, a quick wit and a most personable appearance, he had no difficulty in inspiring confidence and obtaining excellent positions. He always gravitated to rather high-level jobs in which he was responsible for considerable sums of money. For a while he would function with complete reliability, but soon after establishing himself he would begin to devise clever methods of embezzlement. These would succeed for a time, but then, inevitably, he would find himself on the brink of discovery. In desperation he would struggle to hide his acts; he would plead with his wife and friends to help him raise funds to cover what he had taken. Swearing that this was the last time he would do such a thing, he was so convincing, so pitiable, so desperately anxious to save his family from disgrace, that he repeatedly succeeded in extracting sufficient funds from others to cover what he had stolen. This was his pattern, his "fate neurosis," and while he struggled heroically to free himself from its compulsion, the power of his early conditioning was such that he found himself repeating it again and again. Because he did not accept his criminal motivations but fought and was tormented by these childish residues, his was a "neurotic" criminal mechanism.

This man was one of those children who are unwanted from the moment of conception. His parents' marriage was close to the very fringe of that one-third of marriages which end in divorce. They lived together in a state of armed truce, hostile to each other and escaping from each other into outside interests as much as possible. The child was an unhappy accident. But just as the parents did not quite get a divorce, they did not quite get an abortion. Sometimes a child can save a marriage; perhaps this one did, but at an emotional price to itself, the price of emotional deformity.

It was in this ungiving, unloving world of his childhood that he learned to "work" others, to achieve what he could through wit, charm, cajolery. The starving man finds food as best he can; the emotionally starved child struggled for love as best he could. Assuredly man does not live by bread alone.

Many a child tries to stay his emotional hunger by consuming candy. Often he cannot refrain from filching it. Others demand such inadequate substitutes for love as toys or money, and these, too, such children are frequently unable to keep themselves from secretly appropriating. This little boy's father sometimes gave him pennies, dimes and nickels. This was not done in a setting of really interested love, but rather in place of it. Nevertheless, so little attention did the child get from his father that these gifts provided thrilling moments for him. He would literally dream about the small change and, when it was not forthcoming, he gradually learned how to remove some from his father's clothes without being detected.

Soon his whole quivering interplay of emotions began to cluster around this pilfering. Soon the small change represented not only the love and concern he wanted from his parents, but also, by treating his friends, the means for buying love. Through this act he also expressed hatred engendered by the parents' rejection and courted punishment for this hatred. Of course, this tendency for self-punishment was not conscious to him as a child nor as an adult. Even as a grown man he was unable to face the pain of acknowledging to himself how unwanted he was. All he was ever aware of both then and earlier was a Damocles' sense of impending doom, of some unknown sword hanging over him by a thread. This latent guilt and need for punishment, no weaker because not conscious, provided yet another motive for his thefts. Each time he stole and was not caught, he felt a greater reassurance, seeing in his escape the proof that fate, so often seen in the image of the parents, had not after all really abandoned him.

Thus his neurotic criminal behavior came to express emotions too powerful to resist. In adult life, he struggled against them. He was not, like the criminoid character, able to control the direct acting out of his antisocial impulses; but unlike the true criminal, he could not embrace and make a career out of them. Nor were his defenses strong enough to prevent the acting out of his warped, childhood emotional patterns, though they were strong enough to see to it that he punished himself with poignant suffering.

THE NEUROTIC CHARACTER

For a long time, the term "Constitutional psychopathic inferiority," familiarly called "CPI," was used as a frankly catch-all label for behavior disorders which fitted none of the other diagnostic categories. With increasing knowledge of the effects of early conditioning experiences and with the realization that there was at present no valid evidence to support the term "constitutional," that part of the label was dropped, and the term "psychopath" substituted. But as many of these individuals came to be studied psychoanalytically, it was recognized that they were motivated by precisely the same emotional mechanisms which in other persons produce physical and psychological symptoms, and that here was neurosis expressed more in actual behavior than in thought, feeling or bodily organs. Hence the term "neurotic character" was introduced by Franz Alexander.

As we have noted, infantile impulses persist in everyone to some degree. If these have been patterned by basically good relationships and if they are balanced off by mature motivations, then they cause no difficulty. On the other hand, if they have been distorted by conflict-full conditioning, if the person suffered too much emotionally as infant and child, if they have been so intensified that the mature development is hampered, then they will disturb some aspect of the individual's functioning. The neurotic character differs from the criminal, the criminoid and the neurotic criminal in that he defends himself against his infantile hostile impulses in such fashion that, though acted out, they appear only in indirect, disguised form. Essentially he suffers from a *private neurosis*, in which the underlying hostility, while it may affect intimates and other individuals, is repressed and associated with self-induced punishment.

The example we shall present shows an underlying personality structure similar to that of the neurotic criminal described previously. The two histories, however, contrast in certain important details which illustrate the specific quantitative role that early influences play in choice of outcome.

An ambitious, highly intelligent young man had lost his mother through death before he reached the age of one year. The father hired a nurse to care for him, and gave him very little attention or companionship. Meanwhile the nurse answered any childish misbehavior by reminding the growing boy that she was not his mother but was being paid for taking care of him and would leave if he did not act as he should. The combined rejection of both nurse and father filled the child with resentment. Although in childhood, while the ego is weak, feeling is usually almost synonymous with action, this boy strove to repress all retaliative behavior because he feared total abandonment.

How was he able to develop effective enough psychological defenses against his anger, induced by such treatment, to prevent its acting out as criminal tendencies? This was primarily for two reasons: In the first place, in spite of the faulty upbringing, the father and nurse did have considerable affection for the child. The former loved his small son after the fashion of so many busy, self-centered men who find too little time to translate their interest into a real experience for the child. The nurse, too, notwithstanding her terrifying threats to leave, actually stayed on faithfully for many years.

In the second place, as we have mentioned, this boy was so insecure that he dared not put into action his real resentful feelings. Any hostile behavior which would verge in the direction of the criminal was checked by love and by fear. He dared not act in any antisocial way for fear of losing what little emotional support he had, and also, because of loving and being loved to some degree, he repressed the impulses.

Thus the anger, pent up toward his father and nurse, was largely turned against himself; and when one hates those he also loves, guilt is probably inevitable.* The guilt in turn made him feel that he deserved to be rejected and was in reality just as bad as they all suspected. These motivations of hostility and guilt added a new dynamic to the boy's environment. In the emotional life, "the punishment fits the source"—that is, the *punishment takes the form of whatever caused the anger*. In this case, the source or cause was rejection; it caused anger which caused guilt; the guilt led to a desire for punishment in the specific form of being rejected, which led to his unconsciously provoking rejection—a truly neurotic and vicious circle.

As we all do, this boy grew up to expect from other adults the treatment he had received from those nearest him in childhood. He would enter into friendship with a great hunger for the attention he had always sought in vain. But soon he would feel that the other person (like father and nurse) was not really interested in him and did not understand him. Then his underlying feelings of deprivation would be ignited and set off his anger, which

---

* Two mechanisms can be distinguished. The one is the stimulated hostility from the id pent up and turned against the self, presumably by the conscience (more broadly and technically, the superego). The other is hostility to the self which originates in the conscience—blaming oneself for past deeds or current wishes.

How We Handle Our Hostilities

appeared mostly in subtle reproaches against his friend, such as tacitly making him feel that he did not quite live up to expectations. The hostility toward himself came out by continuing these reproaches in a provocative way until the friend actually did lose patience with him. When this occurred, as it did in childhood, he would complain to a new confidant about his disillusionment and betrayal by the former friend. This complaining to another was the nearest he ever came to any direct hostility to anyone other than himself.

Occasionally as he went through the cycle, he did in fact get himself so rejected in spite of conscious efforts to avoid it that the relationship was finally broken off. Usually, however, he would be able to continue a precarious contact with the person from whom he turned in favor of another. And so the relationships of his adult life were of the same tenuous, ambivalent nature as his feelings toward father and nurse in childhood.

This childhood pattern of turning from one to another repeated itself with friends in school and in a whole series of jobs. It also repeated itself with girls. He did marry, but in spite of every attempt to preserve the marriage, his wife could not stand the petty, peevish pattern of provocativeness as it emerged toward her, and in the end she divorced him. With his ego-saving capacity for projection, he convinced himself and also some others that the entire fault lay with her, complaining of her egocentricity and inability to have any real interest in him. By this defense of projection he did not suffer directly from his guilt and kept tolerably comfortable.

In this person, the hostility was rarely expressed in a

direct way. For the most part, it caused guilt and was turned against himself to harm his own life by making himself rejected and isolated, deprived of good, warm feelings for and from other persons. His behavior shows the mechanism of the neurotic character because, while consciously striving to get along with others, the present was unconsciously lived for him by the child within him, conditioned to this pattern during his earliest years. This emotional pattern eventuated in *the way he lived* rather than in specific psychological or physical symptoms as in the classic neuroses. That is the key to the neurotic character.

CLASSIC NEUROSIS

We have noted in passing that if the term "neurotic" is taken in its broadest meaning of any emotionally caused disorder resulting from influences during childhood which block and warp full development, then all of our categories (except certain cases of the "sublimated") are various forms of neurotic disturbance. On the other hand, the word "neurosis" was originally used in a restricted sense to apply to certain symptoms and combinations of them (that is, syndromes), especially those designated as hysteria, phobias and compulsion neurosis. It is these which were particularly studied and elucidated by Freud. As pointed out earlier in this book, the well-known mechanism of neurotic symptom formation is the disguised return from repression of strong, mostly infantile, emotional forces.

Because of the individual's mature drives, his adult

standards, his training and his conscience, these infantile forces are controlled and denied direct expression. But such unrelieved tensions affect the normal mature thought, behavior, vegetative functioning and even sensory perception—that is, they cause symptoms. If the forces of maturity and restraint are inadequate and cannot master or offset the infantile motivations, then we see the mechanisms of criminal acting out of impulse-ridden behavior, of certain perversions, of masochism and of similar deficiencies of mature control. This is not neurosis in the classic and narrow sense of repression by conscience and re-emergence of the repressed infantile impulses as symptoms, but it is neurosis in the broad sense of the same disturbed psychic forces being at work, of adult emotional disorders resulting from *the persistence of disordered childhood patterns*.

To illustrate the dynamics of hostility in classic neurosis, let us select a simple, relatively common type of case and, for variety, one where there is a strong "reactive" element. Here the symptoms result from internal emotions which have been intensified by an external life situation.

A personable young woman came for treatment, complaining of anxiety. This anxiety was without content. She did not know what she was anxious about. But, nevertheless, she lived in a state of persistent fear and felt that this might portend some evil about to befall her family. She was married and had one child. The anxiety, it turned out, had developed in the course of a pregnancy and became much more severe when she left the small town in which she was reared and came with her husband

and new baby to live in the metropolis to which his work brought him. Her anxiety now had mounted to the point where she was quite unable to enjoy anything in her life and began to fear she was headed for a nervous breakdown.

The salient feature of her childhood was overprotection. In common parlance, she had been a "spoiled child." Her parents had seen to it that everything was done for her; even as she grew older her life had been a playtime with practically no responsibility. Both her father and mother were leading citizens in the town, and wherever their daughter went, she was welcomed and treated with deference. She knew "everyone" and "everyone" accepted and knew her.

When she married, however, an extremely common difficulty arose. Shortly after the first baby was born, her husband was promoted and transferred. The only life the young wife had known had been her entirely dependent, protected play-relationship to her parents and to the community in which she grew up. Now she was suddenly removed from this to become, far away, just one of millions. Naturally her husband could not provide all the emotional support which she had left behind. It was a rude awakening for the girl to find that he was not father, mother and friends rolled into one but merely another person of her own generation who had to devote his major time and interest to his job.

Not only was her emotional intake suddenly diminished from a flood to a trickle by the geographical move, but in addition, for the first time in her life, she had to shoulder real responsibilities. Now she had a young baby

How We Handle Our Hostilities

with its enormous demands for time, attention and energy and its relentless interference with her indulgence of herself. In addition to the baby, there was also the house to run, the problems of shopping, cleaning and getting help, to say nothing of the harassments of budget. In other words, the emotional give-get balance had shifted—much less was coming in, much more going out. She was like a little child abandoned by her parents and, to add insult to injury, she even had to be a parent herself while trying to adjust in a new community.

She reacted, as do all animal organisms, with a fight-flight response. She thought of running home to mother; but much as she wanted to, she could not accept this path of action, jeopardizing as it would her marriage and the security of a home for her child. With flight cut off, she felt trapped and her anger mounted. However, this rage at being thus caught could not be expressed either; there was no pattern in her life for that. The anger pent-up inside her was the danger which she sensed; but she was by no means aware of her emotional situation as we have described it. She did not think of herself consciously as a dependent, overprotected child. Neither did she realize the extent to which she protested against the move from home into the responsibilities of husband, home and baby, in a new, strange, distant city.

Repressed hostility is perhaps the commonest single cause of simple anxiety states (anxiety hysteria) like this. At times this young wife occasionally lost her temper with her husband but that was about all the hostility that ever came to the surface. She would have been horrified at the idea of having any resentment against her child and his demands. Thus her own unexpressed rage caused the threat of impending doom.

This is a typical neurotic mechanism. The hostility is defended against and repressed and the individual does not behave violently or antisocially and revenge herself directly upon anyone. But this hostility which is apparently dismissed so effectively does not lose its power. It generates a neurotic symptom: in this case, simple anxiety. This anxiety is basically only a personal symptom but it does affect those with whom the individual is intimate. An anxious wife, unable to enjoy her child and husband, feeling restricted in her activities, is no easy mistress of a household; the husband and child suffer. This is what Freud called "the return of the repressed"—this indirect effect of a repressed motivation.

This type of case is seen so frequently that another characteristic feature is worth mentioning. The repressed hostility may return pointed inward against the person himself, and, directly or through generating unconscious guilt, create needs for self-punishment. Usually the individual then reacts by denying himself relief from the very responsibilities which he protests against. For example, the husband or friends see something of what is going on, as, vaguely, does the young woman herself. They urge her to get some help with house and baby, to get out more, to get her life into balance. But typically, as in this case, the anxiety prevents her from achieving the solution. She fears that if she is away something will befall the child and, by similar motivation and thinking, cuts herself off from the normal satisfactions of recreation, attention and emotional support, which friendly contacts might yield. She becomes caught in an all-too-common vicious circle—frustration → anger → guilt → frustration—and is another example of how "the punishment fits the source."

THE PSYCHOSOMATIC MECHANISM

Throughout our discussion of human personality development, we have seen that man is a biological unit and that when he is under stress, either internal or from without, his functioning is affected. Because he is a well-integrated unit, such stresses are reacted to by the entire organism. In some cases, however, they disturb one area of functioning *more* than another. Insofar as the higher centers of the nervous system are affected, we see manifestations of abnormal perception, thought, feeling or behavior or any combination of these. And insofar as the autonomic nervous system is affected, we see disturbances in the vegetative organs, i.e., psychosomatic symptoms. When disturbed emotionally, each individual reacts characteristically. One may burst out in a childish tantrum, another may be depressed, still another may develop a pain in his stomach, or an asthma attack or heart trouble or a headache. Any and all combinations of reactions and symptoms can occur in a given case, in all areas of functioning, from the highest intellectual level to the lowest, most subtle and most automatic. Even the fragility of certain cells of the blood is reported to alter under stress, emotional or physical.

"Psychosomatic" is a term which, in the author's opinion, is best used in the broad sense of meaning any physical symptom in which emotions are of appreciable causal importance.

At least three mechanisms can operate in the contributions of emotions to symptoms. In the first group are those symptoms which are dramatizations or symbolizations of emotionally charged ideas. An example would be Freud's famous one of the girl who repressed her guilt about making a misstep sexually but expressed it symbolically by dragging her foot. Such a mechanism is that of classic conversion hysteria.

In the second mechanism a particular emotional need is expressed through a particular organ. Franz Alexander in *Psychosomatic Medicine* portrays the best-established example of this: that of hunger for love being expressed through the stomach as hunger for food. Biohistorically, this derives from the child's nursing years when the intake of food is closely associated with the intake of love. Thereby these two hungers seem to become conditioned to each other. Later in life, when the adult craves love, his stomach may react as though it were preparing to receive food. If the need for love is not satisfied and the individual is angered, the anger, too, can affect the function of the stomach. The whole interplay of emotion, then, influences that organ system which chiefly expresses the need.

A third mechanism is that in which the symptom is simply part of the body's normal physiological reaction. When a person or animal is angered, there is regularly, as part of his fight-flight response, an increase in the rate and forcefulness of his heartbeat and an elevation of his blood pressure. These subside, along with the rest of the physiology, when the danger or irritant is past. In some cases, however, these cardiovascular symptoms are observed to occur without adequate external stimulation. In at least some of these cases, they are found to be reactions to anxieties which arise from within. The readying of the physiology for the exertion of fight or flight, of course, occurs regardless of whether the threat, irritation or frustration is from outside or inside.

One may observe this physiological arousal in full or, apparently and for not well understood reasons, only in part. For example, one may see an elevation of blood pressure but few or no other signs of physiological overactivity. In such cases (of essential hypertension) preliminary studies suggest that these persons are usually in a state of intense, constant rage which, although near the surface, is typically well controlled so that their manner may be pleasant and gentle. Here one sees the mechanism of hostility, defended against and repressed, affecting the physiology through a chronic elevation of blood pressure.

Perhaps it is superfluous to recount a specific example of hostility-producing psychosomatic symptoms. Who has never felt an anger within him make his heart pound, his color change, stomach and bowels tense up? Who has never noticed that illnesses in himself and others occur during periods of emotional stress? Hostility in one form or another seems to be of critical importance in many bodily conditions. Some epileptic attacks seem to be massive discharges of rage through muscular convulsions. Hostility seems to play a role, at least in part, in certain cases of hyperthyroidism and diabetes and indeed to some extent (probably because of being part of the fight-flight reaction) in most or all disturbances of the physiology by emotional strains. Here is a case of how it affected a peptic ulcer.

The patient, a college student, was appealing, intelligent and quick to gain insight into her problem. A flare-up of the ulcer from which she had suffered since she was fourteen reportedly brought her in for treatment, but it rapidly became clear that what was chiefly disturbing her was unconscious, inner rage.

Her father, to whom she was deeply attached, had died when she was thirteen. This necessitated the mother's obtaining a job in order to support her three children—the patient, a younger sister and an older brother. When an opportunity was offered the mother in the small town where she had been raised, she took the children there and began a new life.

Thus, precipitously, this girl had lost not only her favorite parent but also her close friends and her whole school environment, all of which meant much to her. Meanwhile, not only had her relationship with her mother never been close, but now her mother, through the loss of her husband and through the emotional drain involved in earning a living, was herself under great stress. Frustrated, uprooted and lonely, the girl became irritable and withdrawn—fight and flight.

At about the same time, she also developed stomach trouble, had a hemorrhage and was rushed to the hospital where it was found she had a peptic ulcer. Under strict medical supervision, she improved and, meanwhile, the mother, feeling more secure and seeing that her child was unable to make an adjustment in the new town, sent her, through the help of a scholarship, to boarding school. Here the girl was much happier and had no further trouble with her stomach until she left to go to college. This move again meant leaving old friends and the security of established ties. She still felt ill at ease with her mother and was unable to talk over her personal problems at home. Her shyness made it difficult for the other students to know her. And so once again she was cut off from her dependent attachments. Her longings were frustrated and intensified and the old reaction occurred—inner rage, withdrawal and a flare-up of the ulcer.

Needless to say, not all ulcers or other physical symptoms are caused by emotional factors alone. In this case, the evidence was cogent: even such a small thing as a disappointing letter from her mother or rejection by an acquaintance would precipitate severe abdominal pain.

She obtained marked relief after a few interviews, for she became rapidly aware of what was going on in her emotions. For the first time in her life, she began to face frankly her deep-seated needs for love and dependence and the hostility aroused in her by the frustration of these. She had not realized the amount of anger bottled up beneath her sense of being lonely and shy. Directed mostly against her mother, it had been too full of conflict for her to face. As she began to become acquainted with these feelings, the conflict moved, as it were, from the physiological level up to the psychological. Instead of being reflected in her stomach, her problem became a matter of comprehensible reactions which she could now understand, deal with and begin to solve. The hostility, too, so long unacknowledged, could be faced as a psychological problem, and as a force within herself which did no good and much harm. The hostility could be reduced by understanding its sources and shifting the attitudes which underlay them. This is not always achieved by insight alone but may require systematic reconditioning by psychoanalysis to correct the childhood pattern as it is transferred to the analyst.

SUBLIMATION

The term "sublimation" was introduced by Freud to signify the transformation of crude, animalistic impulses into socially acceptable and useful drives. As first used by him, it applied chiefly to the libidinal impulses. For example, love, however physical its nucleus, can become the kind of love one bears toward parent, child, country or humanity, and can be expressed in literature and art.

There is, of course, no reason why sublimation should be limited to libidinal impulses. Even direct hostility can be rerouted or transformed within the personality so that it motivates action devoted to the welfare of others. This can occur in a variety of ways.

Freely accepted, overt hostility can be used to attack social evils such as crime or tyranny or in defense of one's home and family. Here the destructive impulse may be retained in its original form and acted out, but its aim is pro-human and constructive.

Secondly, the hostility may not be naked nor expressed in an open fashion, but may be verbal and intellectual rather than physical. To distinguish it more clearly from our first example, contrast the commando or police officer with such a crusader for human rights as Dorothea Lynde Dix. Though physically frail and ailing, she stumped the country, storming the citadels of authority with rousing speeches against those who maltreated the mentally ill.

(And as good an illustration of sublimation of hostility as any is the well-known dodge of giving little Willie, who is smashing the furniture, nails and wood so he can hammer just as freely, but constructively instead of destructively.)

Thirdly, hostility which is quite unconscious and in no way evident may generate *overcompensatory* attitudes or acts of good will which betray their source only when analyzed. This compensatory reaction may be quite successful; it is a mechanism which can underlie such socially useful work as surgery or other humanitarian activities. The surgeon, in addition to his mature motivations, unconsciously *may*, in certain instances, satisfy hostile feelings by cutting human beings, even though, like all physicians dealing with illness, suffering, mutilation and death, he does his work in the service of relieving suffering and prolonging life.

Dynamically speaking, perhaps only the crusader mechanism represents true sublimation in the most precise sense. There is in the others some mixture of rationalization—that is, an ostensible (and often a good) reason masks the deeper, real reasons. This must be distinguished from true sublimation. For instance, conscious rationalization is well known on the international scene. There are countless examples of wars being rationalized by an attacker who consciously and deliberately devises reasons to justify his armed hostile aggression.

The following illustrates sublimation, the hostility here being coupled with a mature drive of responsibility.

A young woman lawyer, with a husband, two children and an excellent practice, was famous for her work among the underprivileged. Not only did she extend them professional aid but she made many personal sacrifices on their behalf, sometimes involving sacrifices from her own family. This drive stemmed in large part from a mature wish to use her own powers and fortunate position to improve the lot of others, reinforced by a number of childish impulses, including a considerable amount of hostility.

The source of hostility was found in her childhood, coupled with the drive for responsibility. She had lost her mother when she was six. This left her, an only girl, with her father and two small brothers; and the father soon came to use her all he could in the care of these younger children. About this she had mixed feelings; in part she deeply resented the burden, but in part it gave her a sense of superiority. There was, of course, considerable hostility to the boys, not only because of having to care for them when she wanted to be free, but also because of rivalry. She felt an intense need to be the first in her father's affection and to hold a favored place as the oldest child against their competition. During the day she managed to put up a brave front, but at night, when she was alone, she would weep, look up at the stars in search of her mother and feel very small, needy, poor and forlorn.

Two mechanisms shaped themselves during these years. First, an *identification* of herself with people who were loaded with responsibilities beyond their ability, people who struggled beyond their strength. The second was *overcompensation* for her competitive-resentful hostility against such weaklings.

These two mechanisms developed this way: She did not dare show any anger toward her brothers or father for fear of losing her father's approval. As a defense, she exaggerated her maternal feelings and behavior toward the brothers. Like herself, the boys were destitute of a giving mother and so, by identifying with them, feeling herself one of them, she was able to enjoy some of the help she gave, vicariously, as though it were help received. Meanwhile, she let out her hostility through her need to be superior and to keep the boys in their place. Through these two devices she gained much satisfaction.

Both patterns functioned similarly in adult life. In helping the underprivileged, she could prove herself secure, worthy of admiration and well placed. Meanwhile she could also satisfy her hostile impulses in an overcompensatory, kindly way through her role as a superior with authority.

The total result was a constructive contribution to the welfare of others although largely supported by sublimated hostility.

Part Four

HOSTILITY AND
EVERYDAY LIVING

6 *Hostility and Politics*

THE POPULATION is a reservoir of hostility, conscious or unconscious. Morality and ethics are not goody-goody, but are the expressions of the mature forces of cooperation upon which society is based, society with all it provides in protection for its members in a hazardous, inexorable universe. Demagogues rise to power chiefly by organizing and manipulating the latent hostility in the body politic. Hence they so often begin with little lies, twists of truth, and other corruptions of morality and ethics, the dikes against the ever-present sea of hostility, seeking to make little cracks which will widen to let through the latent elements of violence and permit criminal and criminoid action without undue hindrance.

We will now concentrate on the personal emotional factors which influence or determine an individual's politics, with no attempt to weigh or judge the reasons, pro and con, of specific political actions, beliefs and behavior.

The sources of political *feelings* lie in childhood, and in general adults repeat on the social scene the pattern of family "government" which they knew in childhood. Various social studies have shown this over and over again. Otto Klineberg's survey of the "Tensions Affecting International Understanding," made for the Social Science Research Council (in New York), for instance, related how authoritarian homes in Germany produced authoritarian (Nazi) adults, while democratic homes produced democratic (anti-Nazi) adults. Anthropological studies sketch the same pattern.

Thus we are safe in saying that democracy, as we desire it consciously, requires first basically democratic homes with each member having his individuality respected, his voice heard, and leadership, but not dictatorship, coming from those most worthy to lead. Neither tyranny by the adults nor tyranny permitted the children can achieve family democracy and mature cooperation.

Looking more closely, there are three fundamental problems which must be met in the course of family development. These are: (1) the child's rivalries with its brothers and sisters, or, if it is an only child, with other children; (2) the child's attraction to and rivalry with its parents, the Oedipal situation; (3) the child's adaptation to his dependent position in the custody of adults, and to the parents' position of power over him.

We have discussed in Chapter 4 the potential tyranny in point three. Let us now look at sibling rivalry and the Oedipal relationship, and their effect on political feelings.

It is very likely that the child's emotional problem of adapting to brothers and sisters is the root of later feelings of need for equality among grown men and women, as Freud suggested in his *Group Psychology and the Psychoanalysis of the Ego*. Children demand equality of treatment from their parents. Hence this demand to be

Hostility and Politics

treated equally in childhood forms a foundation for man's desire for social, political and economic equality.

At the same time the pathology of rivalry with brothers and sisters also may provide the nucleus for pathology in man's later view of social equality. If one child is grossly favored over another, he may turn into a social being who expects, wishes and demands that he himself or his small group be favored over other persons or other groups in society.

Conversely, children who have been rejected often gravitate to the fringes of society, feeling that as they have not been accepted by their own parents they will not be accepted socially. Many of them, as in childhood, yearn for love and acceptance, and seek it, but inexorably following their childhood pattern, never achieve it.

Second, it is probably in the child's relationship to its parents that the hierarchical pattern for all societies has its roots. Freud felt that man's early history of government was a history of paternal despotism. One reason why democracy has been so new and tender and so constantly threatened from within and without may well be because of the despotism which is still exerted within so many homes. Children who come from families in which this is not true will not accept such a society: they say with Abraham Lincoln: "I would be neither slave nor master."

The general political problem which arises from the Oedipus relationship, most clearly seen, perhaps, in that of the boy to his father, is the wish to be like him, to be as the father appears to the small child, big and powerful. The little child tries in many ways to be an adult. If he develops well, if his parents understand and help him with this rivalry as with his sibling rivalry, he will solve it and eventually, as an adult, achieve a mature identification. But such childhood attitudes as dependence, submissiveness and guilt, persisting strongly, make many adults feel anxious and weak and they struggle to "be the father" in their relations with others, to establish a predominant position for themselves, to seek power, with little regard for the realities and needs of other personalities. Unresolved Oedipal relations to the father and the mother thus can become an important enemy of democracy and an aid to dictatorship and regimentation.

These family problems of childhood and the type of solution found by the child form one very important factor in his later social and political reactions and motivations. But other childhood motivations also are of great importance, persisting as they do within the adult and shaping his views and behavior far more than his reason guesses.

For politics serves as an expression not only of a man or woman's immediate estimate of what he wants for his own welfare, but also of his personality make-up. What a man wants for himself, how strongly he wants it, how much he considers others or will sacrifice them, how far he will go with his hostilities to achieve his ends, how clearly he sees that his own well-being is part of his society's well-being—all depends upon the kind of person he is, which results, in turn from his childhood emotional constellation. *There is a dynamics of political feeling which reflects the dynamics of the personality.*

Recently reviewing a series of random examples, I

Hostility and Politics

found they fell roughly into two groups: in one the political feelings resulted from *specific* relationships to the parents or other family members; in the other, they were derived from more *general* emotional dynamics.

As an example of the first, here is the story of two brothers with a colorless, submissive mother and a strict, dominating father whose word was law in the household. As a child the older boy found his modus vivendi with his father through an unquestioning obedience which obviated all conflict with him. As an adult he fully accepted his father's unbending religious orthodoxy, his authoritarian political views and party affiliation, his rigid conventionality. What rebellion he had against the paternal molding was so effectively repressed that no signs of it were discernible. Politically then, he became the complete "follower," a dupe for the demagogue, the power hungry —a man conditioned to regimentation, afraid of equality or democratic expression.

Not so the younger brother. He conformed, but only outwardly. Only a little beneath the surface seethed his rebellion until, just after adolescence, it became openly apparent. He left home and swung to the opposite of his father on all the latter's major issues. He defied convention with wine and women, turned openly against the father's church and swung to the opposite side of the political fence, joining noisy protest groups where he could speak his revolt against anything and everything.

Here, then, are two sons in the same family whose political feelings and identifications are the extreme opposites, but in both there are underlying personality factors which are reactions to a parent. Why these reactions differed in the boys was a matter of specific quantitative difference in the home emotional influences.

Another example is that of a young girl whose mother was one of those forceful widows who take hold of a business on her husband's death and drive on to outstanding financial success, while continuing at the same time to dominate her family. Neglected by her mother, and even resented by her as an interference with her career, the little girl was entrusted to a martinet of a governess who did not hesitate to beat her physically into submission. Probably only a good relationship to a younger brother as a fellow sufferer saved this girl from developing a psychosis as an adult. As it was, she suffered so that when she grew up she spread her feelings of hostility against her mother to include all wealthy people and all successful business people, and politically she became what her mother's friends called "a traitor to her class."

Although in the case of this girl various attempts were made by her family to blame her education and her newfound associates, external elements played a very minor role indeed in her particular political activities. Sometimes, however, they play a stronger role, evoking repressions and regressions that otherwise might be outlived.

For instance, there was the patient who sought help allegedly because of stomach trouble and sleeplessness. He was a young man of high ideals on the threshold of maturity who had entered politics in an effort to break a corrupt machine. The fight involved many men who had little interest in the good of their party, and less, or none, in the welfare of the constituency. He had to work and cooperate with many a criminoid character. He was infuriated by them to the point of losing his appetite for food and sleep. He was mature enough to have a true interest in others, but not mature enough to stand alone and to use all he learned for socially constructive ends. Too indulged in his own childhood, he had tendencies to be criminoid himself, to act for his own advantage, regardless of others. If his associates had been themselves mature and working primarily for the public good, he probably would have identified with them, taken them as models and gradually grown to that stature. Since they were as they were, he was torn between his childish reward-seeking pattern (which he saw motivating so many of them) and his avowed mature drives toward the good of others—not only "the people"—but the office staffs, supporters, friends and even wives and families who were trapped in this battle for prestige and gain.

To illustrate, now, those dynamics which are general and not specific reactions to the politics of the parents, here is the case of a young man, recently married and just embarked upon his career, a kindly person with good feelings for all people. Yet he shows one streak of prejudice against those less fortunate than himself. In analysis it soon appears that he represses and is quite unconscious of an envy of those who have more money and more elaborate homes than he, an envy unreasonable to feel, when he cannot expect at his age the income of those who are much older. (However, the infantile motivations do not respect such realities of time. The child wants what it wants at the moment.) He is not even vaguely conscious of this hostility, born of envy, toward the older men who are his benefactors; he acts in a friendly fashion toward those who could fire him or seriously damage his career, meanwhile projecting his hostility onto those less well off than he.

In them he sees the envious competition which he dares not face in himself, and he fears that they will take away what he has, although it is actually he who wishes to take from them. It does not occur to him that in reality he is closer to the young men in his firm than to his seniors and that they can be his friends in a truer sense than the older men can ever be. In a parallel pattern, his political feeling develops; he distrusts the poor, the foreign, the have-nots and the underdogs and casts his arguments and votes only to aid the successful to be more successful.

A similar mechanism is encountered in some "self-made" men. One who came to me originally for advice about his daughter showed a typical pattern. Although this man wore tailor-made suits, although a chauffeur waited outside for him, although his honors were many and distinguished, he saw himself in his mind's eye still a poverty-stricken immigrant laborer slaving on a menial job, and his envy of those successful people who were now his friends was as intense and competitive as it had been when he was at the bottom of the ladder. But of none of this was he really aware; he repressed it out of shame and guilt. The hostility thus engendered found its outlet only against those who reminded him of his one-time inferiority—the poor and needy—and of the things he could not stand in himself.

This is not the pattern of all self-made men. Many, like Lincoln, are especially understanding toward those who started with them but did not rise as far.

A somewhat different mechanism was seen in a man who was the middle child of a large family and felt he had to compete for any love and attention he might get. Feeling deprived and unwanted he therefore felt an inferiority which he masked with a great show of amiability. As a businessman he continued to strive unremittingly for love, prestige and a feeling of belonging, changing his views and attitudes to suit his associates. Inevitably, this pattern was reflected in his politics. While he was a struggling apartment dweller in the city he identified with the underdog, but when he moved to a fashionable suburb, he unhesitatingly switched his identification and affiliations in efforts to find acceptance (real or imagined) with his neighbors.

Here are two complementary examples of other outcomes of domination in childhood.

"I was a cowed child." Not infrequently does the analyst hear this statement. This patient was a brilliant but unfulfilled man who had grown up an only child, much dominated by his mother and the many women in the family. He recalled several times how, when his grandmother wanted his grandfather to do something and the grandfather did not immediately comply but said he would do it later, the old man would receive a terrible tongue-lashing from the grandmother. This created a great threat to the patient. He felt that "he must comply" and repress all rebellion against his grandmother and his equally strong-willed mother.

He thus lived in constant guilt and fear, and, as a defense, developed an exaggerated need to be very good and very obedient in order to assure himself of his mother's love and avoid punishment by her. So great was this that he could not bear any violence, even in a motion picture.

When he came for help, he was oppressed by a feeling that he must work all the time. He was unable to take even a single day off, not because of a great interest in his work, but because of his fear and sense of obligation. Often he felt as though his mother was standing over him telling him that he must work, work and work. Even the wishes of his wife for a holiday could not help him chase this ghost, this imago.

Because of the passivity of his behavior, he was in no way active politically except in his dreams. In dreams he often projected the power conflict onto the political scene and identified and sympathized with the downtrodden whom he saw as himself in childhood seeking freedom from oppression.

An almost opposite case was a man whose effort to solve the same problem was made by identifying with the oppressor. He projected his mother's domination onto those who were in political power and identified with them, and projected his own submissiveness onto the underdog, whom he felt he must conquer as he himself was conquered. Without complete control, he feared that just as his parents ran his life, so all others might try to do likewise. In other words, he saw the world as he did in childhood—either dominate or be dominated, and he dared not cease to dominate lest he become the one who was dominated. This is typical. Most people see the world in the narrow restricted confines of their childhood rela-

Hostility and Politics 131

tion to parents or sibling, in which they must be on one side or the other.

These examples are meant to illustrate how underlying dynamics of personality can determine a person's political feelings and attitudes. No attempt is made to survey the various specific and general emotional mechanisms. Our attention has been confined to political *feelings,* to the importance of the emotional factors, in particular the deeper, usually more unconscious ones, with no reference to any actual facts of political life and realistic appraisal of them. We have only sought to show how the emotions can affect such attitudes, sometimes working against a man's material advantage, sometimes working for it, but in either case not influenced by primarily rational motives.

Projection, i.e., denying motivations in oneself by attributing them to others, is counteracted in the mature by the sense of reality and even in the immature by experience and knowledge. Groups and nations are hard to know realistically and thus there is little corrective for immature emotionally dictated attitudes. Therefore, as we have noted previously, many can imagine a "foreign" nation or unknown group as having all sorts of strange characteristics and motives, with little appreciation of them as actual persons.

This is illustrated by the following simple clinical example. In this case the projected hostility was directed not to another human being or group, but to a fixed stereotyped notion of an animal which has long served man in this role.

A man with very high standards had quite a fight with

his wife one evening. He retired and dreamed that two snakes were whirling around together. Then one of the snakes came toward the dreamer, who tried to step on it but did so in a clumsy fashion. After telling this dream, he went on to say that snakes were dangerous, venomous and deadly and that one must be sure to destroy them. The two being together made him sure they represented his anger of the night before, concerning which he felt much shame and guilt. He felt that it was awful to fight this way with his wife and that some of the things which he attempted to say, but fortunately did not, were really vicious. In regard to his clumsiness in stepping on the snake in the dream, he thought of his difficulty in actually doing anything like that in reality.

These few associations will suffice us to illustrate the central mechanism of the dream: The patient goes to bed distressed and critical of himself because of the fight with his wife. In the dream he handles this sleep-disturbing stimulus by saying, "No, it is not my wife and me fighting, it is only two snakes. It is not *my* impulses or hers which are dangerous, venomous, deadly and vicious, it is those snakes which are that way." But part of the hostility projected onto the snakes begins to turn toward himself as the snake comes toward him. He seeks to defend himself by stepping on it. Thus by projecting his own vicious impulses onto the snakes, he justifies his hostility to them and his impulse to destroy them.

Obviously his prejudice against snakes is shared by many people. The fact is that most snakes are friends of man. They keep down rats and other rodents which carry diseases extremely dangerous to human beings. They provide skins which are useful for making shoes, bags and other objects. Most species are easily domesticated; people who know snakes even have them as pets. All this shows how unrealistic the idea is that all snakes are deadly and must be destroyed. This is a stereotype akin to our stereotypes about alien groups. We fail through our own illusions and projections to see the actual reality and to discriminate between snakes which are dangerous and snakes which are friends to man.

From the author's clinical observation the dynamics of emotional "leftism" or "rightism" seem to be as follows: The emotional rightist projects his feelings of inferiority and his hostilities upon the underdog. Hence he sees the underdog as representing these impulses which are in himself, but which he denies in himself, and sees only in the underdog. The underdog therefore represents to the emotional rightist all that is to be rejected, despised, hostile and feared. The emotional leftist, on the other hand, through his own feelings of inferiority, identifies with the underdog, and projects his egotism, needs for power, graspingness and hostility onto the top dog. Thus the top dog, with whom he does not identify, tends to represent these rejected impulses within himself and he feels oppression by him and envy and hostility toward him. The childhood pattern is usually not far to seek.

These closely related but antithetical mechanisms are represented in two typical dream characters. In emotional rightists, these dream figures, which of course differ widely in details, seem to show the same basic mechanism. Here is one such dream: A poor old creature is working hard and has with him a poorly paid "underdog" assistant who is of little help. The rightist's associations with these figures have to do with his efforts to identify with those who have wealth, fame and prestige; the dreamer goes in for large, expensive automobiles; he looks down upon those who are poor and belong to minority groups; but it soon appears from his associations that he fights off a tendency to identify with the underdogs whom he represents in his dreams. He actually feels inferior to those with wealth, power and position but denies this to himself in his efforts to feel that he is one of them. In so doing, he projects his inferiority feeling upon the less fortunate and the minorities and feels that they want to take away what he himself has and are envious and hostile toward him. By this projection he denies his envy and hostility of those who seem to him to have more wealth and prestige than himself and asserts his superiority, power and hostility toward those he sees as beneath him. Since childhood this man has always been fearsome and angry lest others get something more or better than he.

The opposite mechanism is that of the emotional leftist. In his dreams he is only a menial assistant working hard and getting little in return while an older figure is sitting back doing nothing but being waited upon, and is often in the process of enjoying a sumptuous meal. Here the dreamer attributes to the older man all the gratifications which he himself wants while the dreamer's lot is only to work for him basely, and to be exploited by him. He denies his own wishes for power, prestige, wealth and self-indulgence at the expense of others and projects these desires onto the other man; he also projects his hostilities onto the other man and feels abused, depreciated and taken advantage of by him.

The ideal situation is for each individual to be so mature that he understands his own motivations and those of others realistically and has humanitarian feeling not only for himself and his family, but for all people. He is therefore relatively freed from projections and stereotypes. This is the emotional essence of democracy, as it is of Judeo-Christian morality. It is our chief hope in resolving hostility. It is interesting in therapy to see how this political objectivity can grow as mature feelings develop in analyses undertaken for quite different purposes.

A young lawyer, for example, felt that some analytic work would help him in his human relations and in his profession of the law. Although a pleasant person, others tended to stand off somewhat from intimacy with him, and, to his surprise, considered him cold and unsympathetic. Politics played no role at first in his associations except during an election when there appeared in his dreams certain prejudices of which he was ashamed. Then came some sessions in which the material revealed a strong graspingness against which he sought to defend himself by pointing it out in others. Now he began to see why others treated him coldly, but he had further to go.

He dreamed of being analyzed on a very wide couch on which there were several other people. Then there was an atom bomb exploding while he and they all ran for shelter.

He went on to associate to the first dream:—most annoying to have other people analyzed at the same time—

he wants the analyst's exclusive attention—and interest —as a child he was the oldest of four—he felt he was his parents' favorite—but he had to struggle to keep this position—he always felt his younger brothers and sisters would take away his toys and his favored place. This reminds him of some views he recently expressed about other young lawyers—feelings that they will take over too much practice and get positions he wants—he unhappily admits his feelings of satisfaction that one of them is out with a prolonged illness—this, he sees, is irrational since he himself has an ample practice and is not striving for any particular position—this reminds him of persons of foreign extraction whom he has met. And then, suddenly, he says: "Now I see the connection of all this not only with my friends but with my politics—I have not been really interested in the welfare of people—without realizing it, I have felt as though struggling lawyers and minority groups were like younger brothers and sisters, that they would take away my position and income, and had to be kept down and defended against—I've been the one who's been grabbing all I could and I've felt they were the grabbers who would get things away from me— and the second dream of the bomb must be an unconscious wish for war to destroy these people whom I see as competitors—yet I'm trying to grab for myself—I needn't —I'm doing good work and earning enough. This certainly has not been good will on my part, not any real interest in the welfare of either people in general or of the whole country—it's not been realistic or mature."

This man was fortunate in seeking and finding new growth. Many are not so fortunate. The psychodynamic mechanisms involved in determining the direction and form of politico-emotional feelings are of great significance. But the basic problem is the hostility, the symptom of psychopathology, the force which warps the grasp of reality, impairs identification and fellow feeling, and prevents the shaping of societies without mass cruelty and destruction.

7 *Hostility and Religion*

In his *General Introduction to Psychoanalysis*, Freud said that the three great blows to human vanity were the discovery that the earth is not the center, but only a tiny part of the universe, that man is related to the animals and that unconscious forces so predominantly live our lives for us.

This vulnerable vanity of men, this narcissism and false pride, is infantile in origin and nature. When the tiny, weak, helpless baby, center of its parents' attention, carries these egocentric proclivities full strength into adult life, they become the chief obstacles to mature functioning and happiness on all levels—physical, psychological and spiritual—and a source of conflict and hostility. A relatively mature human being would not feel such facts as threats to his self-esteem but might well feel the opposite: a thrilling sense of significance in being part of so infinite a scheme.

Hostility and maturity are intimately interrelated with all areas of living and particularly with the spiritual-religious aspects of life. The word "religious" is used herein not in connection with religious faiths or sects, but in terms of religious *feelings*. Our concern moreover is with only one aspect of these—their relationship to mature bio-psycho-sociologic motivations; we are not concerned with the various forms of expression in the different churches and denominations.

Religion would seem to involve at least five essentials: (1) a cosmology, (2) rituals, (3) theological systems and doctrines, (4) ethical and moral principles and (5) a relationship to divinity. It is the two latter which concern us here. The cosmology consists of explanations of the origin of the universe, of man and woman, and so on. These explanations are mostly ideational and factual and hence alterable in the light of increasing scientifically established knowledge. The rituals serve very important purposes (such as bringing people together in a common experience, to mention only one), but alone they can become form rather than content and can even be used as a substitute for the content—"for the letter killeth but the spirit giveth life." Theological systems and doctrines are the outward, organized outlets for expression of religious feeling. With ethics and with feelings for divinity, however, we deal with biopsychological connections which are basic in themselves and which bear an important relationship to hostility and to maturity.

Much misunderstanding has been generated about the attitudes of psychiatry toward religion because Freud's initial penetrations into the causes of emotional disorders concentrated on the importance of the sexual motivations. He broadened the concept, as we have noted previously, far beyond sensuality, to cover love in its most sublimated forms and, in fact, practically all positive feelings between people; but many ignored this and misunderstood the sum total of his views as carnal pansexualism. This, plus the vulgar misinterpretation of his descriptions of repression as license to sensuality, resulted in a gross misconception of Freud and of psychoanalysis as antimoral, libertine and anti-Christ.

The reality is precisely the opposite. In his personal life, Freud was puritanically moral, as were his scientific conclusions, namely, that the whole course of the libidinal development consists in outgrowing childish egocentricity and achieving the capacity for unselfish responsible love. This is the essence of his libido theory. Mental disorder, he said, is a matter of libidinal fixations, caused by faulty upbringing during the earliest formative years; it is in essence the result of a failure to lose oneself sufficiently to be able to love.

The striking point is that this conclusion, which has been amply confirmed by later analysts, is identical with that of Moses, Jesus and other great religious leaders. Thus depth psychology, by a totally different route, came, millennia later, to the same "commandments" as Judeo-Christianity and other great religions: for a good, rich and long life man must reduce hostility and love fully.

Yet on second thought this identity in the teachings of science and religion is not striking at all! For it signifies the confirmation, by painstaking scientific work, of realities long divined and felt to be true by the mass of people. Moreover, with recent discoveries of the biological drive toward cooperation, we can now say we have the beginnings of a scientific base for morals and ethics.

It is hardly necessary to state in detail how it is that dynamic psychiatry has reached this moral outcome, for all that has gone before in this book shows that the path

Hostility and Religion

from infantile egoism to relatively unselfish, responsible, productive love is the path to emotional maturity. Put conversely, *failure to mature properly emotionally is the basic source of hostility and of deficient capacity to love. Excess of hate over love is a sign of emotional disorder, the result of warping in the emotional development.* The adult who matures fully is characterized by minimal internal tension, friction, frustration, and hence by minimal hostility and by maximal capacity for forgetting himself and his own childish egoistic demands in favor of loving freely, responsibly, productively, his family and his work, his friends and groups, his nation and humanity.

At medical school one learns that the doctor's task is to help make the bodily condition such that the curative powers of nature can heal most effectively. The doctor's power comes from going along with nature. The doctor himself is evolved by society as part of people's adaptation to nature and he is himself part of nature's process of healing and prevention.

This is undoubtedly why for so long religious leaders have been called "healers." The underlying truth is that health of both mind and body (full "psychosomatic" health, to use the current term) depends upon the harmonious development and operation of all the motivations, and anyone who helps people to the fundamentally proper ways of life in keeping with the deeper motivations of nature is thereby helping people to mental, bodily and spiritual-emotional health. It is foolish to think of science and religion as being at loggerheads—and untrue. The doctor and the "healer" have the same goal—the well-being of man.

Moreover, if the feeling of relationship to divinity does consist in part at least of a sense of closeness to and realization of nature's power and wisdom, and *particularly of the forces which motivate mature behavior,* then many diverse phenomena between religion and science become more intelligible. There is nothing new or revolutionary in this psychiatric approach except the specific importance of the mature drives. And even these findings have been expressed in different idioms before. For instance:

"When I was a child," wrote St. Paul, "I spoke as a child, I understood as a child, I thought as a child; but when I became a man, I put away childish things. For now we see through a glass, darkly; but then face to face. . . ."

Is not one meaning of this that the child is closer to divinity because it is closer to the forces of nature, those within it, those it relates to in nature, and those in its relations with the persons who rear it? Does the reader not remember the freshness of his own feelings in early childhood, his closeness to other forms of life, and to the ocean, mountains, stars. Later this becomes blurred by faulty upbringing and overlaid by the distracting hurly-burly of life, the endless daily pressures which keep us from that early communion with nature, of which we are, however tiny, yet a part.

And St. Paul goes on to say that of faith, hope and love (charity), the greatest is love.

In clinical practice, where analytic treatment is successful, the emotional development is unblocked and hence moves toward increasing energy, freedom and enjoyment of the mature responsible-productive-independent (RPI)

Hostility and Religion

drives, and the ability to love is increased. This ability, this growth toward emotional maturity in compassion and understanding, seems properly designated as "spiritual" growth. And the sense and feeling of the mature motivations in relation to others and to the rest of nature seems to be one component at least of what we remark as spiritual and religious feeling.

Anyone who tries honestly to understand himself and others must realize that his ego perceives the interplay of motivations within his own mind, welling up from his own body and reacted to in accordance with his own early conditioning and his present situation in life. The other person's ego then perceives these interactions in the forms specific for himself. If we could devise a modified and vastly more effective electro-encephalograph, we could "tune in" to the other person's brain and experience in our consciousness what he is experiencing in his. How humble this should make us—and how considerate! For it would emphasize how there, but for the grace of God, go I.

Analytic treatment is successful if it softens the infantile patterns sufficiently for the person to mature through living—to be able to base his happiness, success and security on enjoying love, work and cooperation. As in the rest of medicine, the analyst opens the way for the forces of nature to work the cure. Of course, this can also happen without benefit of analysis.

A striking example of the latter is found in the life story of one of my friends who struggled for years to make money for himself and for his wife and children. But for all his struggles, he did not prosper. At the same time, however, people occasionally came to him seeking the products of what he thought was an utterly unprofitable side line of his failing business. He devoted himself to them freely, merely as a service, without thought of return. The people felt his interest, his willingness, his helpfulness, his "love." They returned and more came, many of whom forced payment on him. Slowly this man became aware of the fact that when he worked for himself, when he directly sought money and financial "success," he failed, but when he stood aside and gave to others, he prospered.

Analyzing himself, he decided that when his primary motivations were grasping, egocentric, infantile, he got nowhere, but when, in spite of these conscious efforts, his mature drives took over and found expression, then these mature drives—his giving, helping, "loving"—won him respect, esteem and financial reward. He reacted to this insight with great humility, realizing that his good fortune had come in spite of his egotism—and he became "religious" in a true sense: he developed a "spiritual" quality. He encouraged his closeness to and recognition of a force within him greater than his own ego: his capacity to lose himself in his interest in others, and thus, by losing himself, he found himself and released his mature powers. He felt awe and realized himself as part of humanity, of all life, of all nature.

We have all had similar experiences, wherein certain men and women impress us as deeply and genuinely spiritual and religious in the best meaning of the term, even though we know little or nothing of their theological beliefs. They are usually persons of insight, depth

Hostility and Religion 145

of feeling and human understanding, and have a close and profound sense of their place in human affairs and in nature. They have found the forces of mature motivations within themselves—the secret of cooperation with nature and man.

Was not Thomas Jefferson such a person? As a youth he was one of the wealthiest men in Virginia and had the means to gratify all his immature desires for egotism, prestige, self-indulgence, as do so many young men of premature wealth, often to the ruin of their lives and those of their families. Instead he dedicated himself to public service and, probably more than any other man in our history, was responsible for the formulation and acceptance of the basic principles of democracy—the Declaration of Independence, the Virginia Statute of Religious Freedom, the foundations of the public-school system and university education, and, largely, for the Bill of Rights. To these great ends he devoted his energies and his wealth. Mature motivations dominated his living.

No doubt many a man is also spiritual and religious in feeling but does not have the same talents as a Thomas Jefferson or an Abraham Lincoln, does not so fit to the needs of the times, and is not tossed by the innumerable determinants into a position in which he can be equally effective and renowned. But even when such men are found in humble stations of life, they are recognized. The truly great, wherever stationed, are humble, and fame is to them only a secondary satisfaction, only, so to speak, the gravy, not the main course. They are not *proud* of their achievements, but find satisfaction in what they have contributed.

Dostoyevsky is one of the Titans of literature. He seems to have had a spiritual quality and a truly religious sense and in him, too, this quality and sense seem to express an unusual sensitivity to motivation, particularly to the mature forces. As Freud noted, Dostoyevsky's hypersensitivity resulted in all likelihood from the anguish of his own severe personal emotional disorders; his interest in hate and suffering and his fight against these and longings to love and be loved probably stemmed largely from the cruelty of his father toward him when he was a youth. But it was not his neurotic problems, but his mature drives, which made possible his capacity for intense interest in man and productive work. "I cannot and will not believe that evil is the normal condition of mankind," he wrote. And he could express the central issue of human life as simply as this: ". . . everyone . . . is wanted." And: "The chief thing is to love others like yourself, that's the great thing and that's everything; nothing else is wanted. . . ." (From Dostoyevsky's short story "The Dream of a Ridiculous Man.")

Thus religious *feeling* seems related to a depth of and closeness to maturity of motivation. It involves first, humility—a consciousness of the self as one tiny expression of the forces of nature which underlie the whole universe and operate inexorably in each of us, and, secondly, the ability to love or a predominance in a person's life of the maturer, more selfless motivations. Both of these demand a *freeing* of the mind from exaggerated or otherwise disordered infantile motivations and both result in the *freeing* of the *creative* forces. This "increase of free energy" and "the reopening of the emotional development to maturity" are two of the common ways of stating the goals of sound analytic treatment.

Both are similarly sought and expected by the great religions and the difference between the scientific and religious formulations resolves itself into one of idiom. Is not the goal of freeing one's mature powers from infantile egocentricity poignantly expressed as: "For whosoever will save his life shall lose it: and whosoever will lose his life for My sake shall find it"?

Some examples of how the basic realities of existence can be expressed in both the idioms of science and of religion are found in a small volume by Rufus Jones, *The Faith and Practice of the Quakers.*

Rufus Jones points out that religious truth must be unequivocally *the truth,* and must not be influenced by prevailing views any more than truth in physics or in medicine should be so influenced.

He continues: Christ's way of life, to which he called his followers, "reverses competition and self-seeking. It trusts to the constructive power of love and cooperation. Consecration to the life of others, self-giving . . . are the very heart of it. The building of the new order of humanity, not by the propagation of a theory, but by the practice of the spirit of consecration and self-giving is, then, at least a possible meaning of the kingdom. . . .

"If we could realize once more, as Clement of Alexandria did in the third century, that salvation is complete spiritual health, we should take a long step forward toward the building of a Church occupied with the tasks of remaking and transforming human life and human society. . . .

"The thoughtful person of our time," Jones points out, "does not look for divinity in origin but in processes, developments, achievement, effectiveness. . . .

"One could see, in addition to the ocean of darkness and death in the world also that of light and love. Under the influences of such experiences and convictions, a person could change from a weak and timorous youth to a robust and fearless adult."

God's will in the soul of man might be translated to scientific idiom: The revelation of nature's forces toward mature behavior, the being at one with the purposes of nature as they operate in adult human beings. "The idea of innate sin in the newborn could be answered by pointing out the presence of the seed or light of God," this being in its description quite equivalent to the seed of mature, loving, constructive behavior. In this sense "religion rests as a last resort not on a book or a church but on the fundamental nature of man's inner being."

Jones finds it "useless now to debate the question whether that divine trait belongs essentially to the human soul or is something supernaturally added to it as a free act of God." Certainly apart from this at present unanswerable question, there seems little in man and the universe upon which science and religion cannot agree if only each is mature enough to be tolerant of the idiom in which the other expresses the truths it sees and feels.

Since religion in so large part reflects man's biological need for *proper direction* and *inner security* in his life, it is doubtful whether good psychiatry and good religion are sharply distinguishable. Both deal with the human spirit; and the troubled spirit seeks peace and strength.

Hostility and Religion

The good psychiatrist cannot be a cold technician. Like any good physician, he must have a spiritual quality himself, an understanding, human sympathy, the free capacity for loving others. The same applies to the good minister who seeks to heal by dealing with motivations and helping sufferers to love. Historically, both were one profession in the ancient days—before medicine separated gradually to find its way back by way of science to dealing with the spirit through dynamic psychiatry. In this sense, psychiatry is an instrument of religious feeling, of man's efforts to comprehend the forces of nature and the goals of mature living and to find his place in the universe.

Hostility and brutality, covert and subtle or open and direct, is the true devil—the sure sign that something has gone awry in the processes of maturing. Instead of love there is hate. Hate is the force that comes to expression in all the bestiality of war. This hostility is the central problem for religion as it is for science. Assuredly science and religion should help each other in combating hostility—this symptom of man's emotional deformity, this mental disease which imposes such worldwide misery and now threatens humanity's very existence.

People do not know their own best interests, largely because of shortsightedness. The childish impulses to *immediate* grabbing readily blind us to what in the not-so-much-longer run makes a good personal life and a good society. Constructive, sympathetic interest in others and in the welfare of all would provide security and direction, harmony with the forces of maturity, and a richer personal life materially and emotionally for all. It is the natural result of proper child rearing.

8   *Hostility and Happiness*

Love appears to be vital to happiness, but hostility and happiness appear to be inconsonant and incompatible. In fact, even a small amount of hostility can be threatening. This is seen in well-meaning, well-intentioned people who repress their hostilities and attempt to lead loving, generous lives of achievement. Without doubt this repression is far better for society as a whole than the criminal and criminoid acting out of hostility, but the nature of hostility is such that completely successful repression is probably not possible. *Thus the "good" may do indirectly what the "bad" do directly.*

For example: An attractive girl of twenty-one was causing her parents much anguish over her sexual behavior. She herself said she saw nothing wrong with it. Her parents, however, could not reconcile themselves to her admission that she had had sexual affairs with several men, changing her lovers every few months. They were shocked at her bohemian way of life with its flouting of convention. The girl was willing to see a psychiatrist only to humor the parents. Her attitude was very simple. She pointed out that she was young; she did not want to get married and settle down immediately; she had strong

Hostility and Happiness

sexual feelings and wishes for love and she did not see why she could not have her "fun." Convention was "stuffy" and she saw much to recommend freedom. She was very direct and forthright and superficially "happy."

At first, she discussed her parents with great objectivity; she said she loved them but felt they simply didn't understand life. As she described her growing up, however, she became more heated. She described them, and especially her father, as being suspicious and impossibly strict in their standards of behavior. She said she felt under constant pressure from them and continually under the imposition of their ideas of what her life should be, that they attempted to handpick her friends, her recreations, and demanded exact obedience as to the hours she came in and where she went. "They treat me like a baby," she said indignantly.

It soon became apparent that it was in self-defense that she had developed a fight-flight reaction; without it, she felt unconsciously that she could not preserve the identity and independence of her own personality. The rebellion, of course, was aimed—again unconsciously—at the very heart of the parents' wishes for her. Since they tried to *compel* her to a rigid "goodness," she sought a defiant pattern of "badness" as an outlet for her hostility.

The parents' protectiveness was born out of love for their child, although a fearful sort of love. It did not take long for the daughter to learn that the chief motivation for her bohemian way of life was as an unconscious means of rebelling, asserting her independence and revenging herself on her parents. She then realized it was a sign that she was not yet a free adult, emancipated from childhood conflict with them, however much she acted as if she were. Once this hostile pattern became apparent to her she saw that a way of life based on hostility would not be happy—that she was, in essence, destroying the very love and freedom she sought by misuse of her sexual drive for an ulterior purpose.

The rebellion against parents' demands takes various forms, and is usually directed very precisely to these demands. When the desire for the success of the child is born of social snobbishness and social climbing, when hostility is generated toward the parents on this count, then the children often behave in ways utterly to outrage the parents socially. They unconsciously choose as friends and acquaintances persons devoid of polish and graces and antipathetic to them, often, indeed, to the point of being personally obnoxious in bearing, dress, speech, manner and conduct. The children unconsciously gravitate toward such acquaintances, friends, lovers, and husbands and wives, thus striking their parents precisely at their weakest spot.

In other cases, one or both parents may place all emphasis upon athletic success. Then the child's rebellion takes the form of a complete disinterest in sports and a shunning of even the most ordinary games. And it is very common to see children, up through college age, who have brilliant intellects, but who fail in their studies out of unconscious rebellion against the prodding of parental demands for grades and competitive success, whether these demands are current or were inculcated during the child's earliest years.

Hostility and Happiness

The precision with which this mechanism operates is very striking. All of us who are parents have seen it in action to greater or lesser degree. What is not so striking at first glance, however, is that the hostility engendered is two-pronged, and aimed not only at punishing the parent, but also at punishing the individual himself.

Parents desiring deeply their children's success in any form of endeavor usually have no conscious intention of using the children as pawns in their own dreams; usually they sincerely love their children and wish them happiness as they see it. As a result, the children usually have a basically sincere feeling of love for them in return and no conscious wish to hurt them.

Therefore the hostility arising in the children against impositions and deprivations bring with them considerable guilt. The guilt, in turn, creates a need on the children's part for self-punishment. The resulting rebellious behavior then serves two needs: attack on the parents and punishment for themselves. The whole process is usually acted out quite unconsciously. In cases that are spotted early enough, the untangling process is fairly rapid and easy, especially when the love overbalances the hate. Often intellectual insight into the punishing behavior reveals it as just a weapon, and not something that is a major personality component, and with this knowledge there may come enough freedom to permit new growth and fresh patterns.

When the love overbalances the hostility and when the hostile self-punishing behavior is just a weapon, then frequently intellectual insight brings with it enough freedom to permit new growth and fresh patterns. But if the pattern is deep seated in the personality, a systematic analytic type therapy will probably be indicated.

Behavior based on hostility is apt to carry with it no real "thrill of achievement," no long-term satisfaction—but new anxiety and new hostility, leading often to a sense of futility.

Our examples were drawn from post-adolescents, but the return of the repressed is a general human phenomenon which occurs in all ages. Poetic justice operates here with *unerring precision:* the punishment is regularly directed to the desire that is the source of the hostility.

We have touched upon two points of such importance for understanding how hostility affects our lives that they require explicit clarification:

The first of these we have referred to as *The good do indirectly what the bad do directly* (with apologies to Plato, who said the good dream what the wicked do). Because what is repressed from consciousness usually or always returns to find some form of expression, hostility that is repressed usually is somehow vented indirectly. The adolescents mentioned above were consciously and patently dutiful, devoted children. They did not explode openly at their parents. But their underlying resentment came out indirectly in disorders of the love-life, of social relations, or in failures in athletics or studies, failures which were unwittingly acted out in order to hurt the parents.

A corollary to this is that the guilt which is so regularly observed is usually not alone for unconscious impulses (as generally described in the analytic literature) which never come through into action. In most cases the guilt is for *actual behavior* even though the hostile meaning of this behavior is not known to the person himself. Again and again one hears of psychologically painful symptoms—and usually finds that what keeps them going is in some part guilt for what the sufferer is indirectly but actually doing to others. It may be to a tyrannical wife and mother, or to a hostilely competitive brother, or whomsoever, but real suffering is caused others however unintentionally.

This guilt for unconscious and indirect although actual hostile behavior causes tendencies to self-punishment. This need for punishment takes many forms—vague anxiety, a sense of impending harm, excessive fearsomeness for self or others, compulsions which curtail free living, depression, ideas of being persecuted, causing oneself accidental injuries—in fact, the whole gamut of psychopathological symptoms; for guilt and self-punishment are probable critical components in all of them, being reactions to the ever-central underlying fight-flight reaction.

The form taken by the self-punishment is of course not accidental, but specifically determined. This brings us to our second point: *The punishment fits the source*. This means that the punishment regularly takes the form of the desire which, frustrated, generates the anger and hostility. A young man, doted on as an only child, strives for prestige, feels dissatisfied and enraged by his failure to gain all the esteem he desires, hating others out of envy for this. His punishment is in the form of defeating his own strivings, so that he may go down instead of up his ladder of success. A woman, rejected in childhood, craves love, but continues her childhood feelings of being unwanted. This enrages her. She hides her hostility, is tormented with guilt, and punishes herself by behavior which estranges the very persons whose love she craves. Dreams are, as Freud said, the royal road to the unconscious. In the dream our true motivations are laid bare in disguised form. The young man had repeated dreams of climbing a cliff but slipping down into a mine shaft. The woman dreamed that people she clung to always left her and she was alone.

It was at once clear that here was a man defeating himself and, through anxieties about his health and work, driving himself toward failure by a self-punishing mechanism.

What was the crime that brought about his sense of guilt? He was charming, well-educated, and on the surface upright and conscientious. It seemed, however, that he had always been what he described as "too attractive to women." As a young man, he had been engaged to several girls but had broken off these engagements on one pretext or another before finally, with reluctance, he married a suitable, lovely girl with whom, almost from his wedding day, he was dissatisfied. Four children were born to their marriage and this further irritated him. He resented helping around the house, taking any authority over the children, playing with them or even taking them on a holiday. In fact, the only pleasure he seemed to enjoy during this period was a series of flirtations with other women, for none of whom he formed any real attachment. In due course, he met a girl who was extremely well-to-do; he divorced his first wife, and married her. While he was aware that he had not loved either of his wives very deeply, he placed all the blame upon them for his lack of happiness.

Superior as he was intellectually, he was completely unaware of the hostility in his life, which resulted chiefly from deep inner protest against any responsibilities and demands upon him. He saw himself as considerate and thoughtful and never visualized the load of guilt and resentment he carried because of hating to give any love and responsible effort.

Bit by bit, in the analysis, the source of his hostility was uncovered. His mother had been an extraordinarily beautiful and vain woman who had asked nothing from him, her only son, but praise and flattery. Preening herself in front of him in pretty new dresses and jewels, she rewarded his admiration with kisses and then left him to baby sitters and maids to entertain himself while she went out. She was not a malicious or mean woman, apparently, but simply a careless, childish one and so, as her son grew, and he began to dislike the emptiness of their relationship, he repressed his hostility toward her and turned it inward on himself.

Because he had inherited her good looks and copied her charm, he was successful in attracting much more love and attention than he might otherwise have received, but because of his inability to return it, he was not successful in keeping it. This, of course, increased his unconscious hostility, which in turn built up more guilt, and eventually demanded active punishment: real loss of love and responsibility, the very things which in his childhood relationship with his mother had caused the trouble in the first place. In him, as in so many, *the punishment fitted the source of the hostile reaction.*

This mechanism elucidates a number of conditions. Freud described several mechanisms for paranoid jealousy, to which this principle adds another. A patient's wife had a lover. The patient repeatedly dreamed that the wife went off with this lover or with other men. Sometimes she died or was killed. The wish was ego-alien, and he awakened with tears and terror. In reality he loved his wife and was devastated by her behavior. Why did he not dream therefore that she gave up the other man, returned to himself and that they lived happily ever after? He was burdened with too much guilt to do this. He loved his wife but also was enraged at her for her attentions to another man, and out of guilt punished himself for this hostility by tormenting himself with the source of it, the jealousy. His wife was unfaithful—he was angered at her—he was guilty for this—he punished himself and the punishment struck at the source; he hated her because of his jealousy and therefore deserved to be made jealous. The hostility must be repressed. It was turned against himself to take this specific form; it was directed at the feeling which was the source of the hostility: the jealousy.

The pattern was laid in childhood. This man's mother had had a lover for whom the children were often neglected. The patient's hostility to her generated guilt and the superego reaction: "Because I hate my mother, I deserve that kind of a wife." Crime: hostility to mother, out of jealousy. *Source* of crime: wishes for mother's

Hostility and Happiness 159

exclusive love. How the punishment fits the source: the inflicting of suffering through not having this exclusive love but faithlessness.

This mechanism also puts "castration anxiety" in a slightly different light. It is well known that in dreams and fantasies, as in disorders of behavior, hostility and guilt are often directed toward the male genital organs. We have touched upon other reasons for this, the simple erotization or sexualization or fusion of hostility, whether directed toward others or the self, with genital sexual feelings. Where the emotional interplay involves predominantly the genital system, then we expect any conflicts to be fought out over this system. Thus, where genital desires are the source feelings, then whatever motives, frustrations and fight-flight reactions result from these, the punishment (i.e., the superego reaction) would be expected to be directed to the source, the genital, thereby causing castration anxiety. Similarly, where the source of the hostility is masculine competitiveness, symbolized unconsciously by size of phallus, then the hostility is in the symbolic form of castrativeness to the envied competitor, and the punishment is fear of retaliation in kind.

That *the punishment fits the source* thus appears to be a general principle and the following phenomenon seems to be an expression of it. Insofar as an underlying need, tendency, wish, desire, seeks expression over a certain pathway, *whether physiological or psychological*, then any resulting conflict, however else it may also be expressed, is fought out over this pathway and all the feelings aroused affect it. This more special principle, the corollary of the general one that the punishment fits the source, is that insofar as the conflict involves hostility and consequent needs for punishment, the punishment is directed to the underlying desires which are expressed over this pathway and affect the pathway itself.

To sum up then: Practically speaking, if a patient complains of inability to be adequately loved, one must suspect that this person is guilty over anger at being denied love and is caught in the mechanism of unconscious self-punishment by denying to himself (or herself) the very love that is craved. Since there are many psychological mechanisms for producing symptoms, and this is only one of them, other mechanisms must be sought, too. But this is so fundamental and so regularly observable that it must always be looked for and never overlooked.

It is better for society and hence for humanity to repress hostility, but this alone is no final, enduring answer for the individual or the race. The return of the hostility, the resulting guilt, the motivations to self-punishment, comprise a major mechanism by which a childhood pattern comes into dynamic equilibrium and persists for life.

Part Five

PREVENTION AND CURE

"If we had just one generation of properly born, adequately educated, healthy children, developed in character, we would have Utopia itself."

HERBERT CLARK HOOVER

9 *Hostility Begins at Home*

EVERY ADULT individual is motivated simultaneously by two sets of forces operating, as it were, on two levels: the conscious and reasonable—and the unconscious and irrational. The conscious and reasonable forces are in general the more mature; the irrational are essentially residues of childish reactions which, disturbed in development, furnish the source for neuroses, psychoses, illness, crime and war.

Mature love can be counted among the rational needs and drives of man. Hostility cannot.

Let us remind ourselves of what was stressed in earlier chapters. Of itself hostility is not a disorder or disease. It is part of a basic biological adaptive mechanism—to meet threats, irritations and frustrations by withdrawing from them or by destroying them. Three main situations make the hostility pathological. If the hostility is kept aroused by the effects of the person's upbringing, by inner anxieties and frustrations caused by this upbringing, by warpings and blocks in the emotional development, then the hostility serves no good purpose; it is a futile, impotent rage which never encounters the real enemy. Secondly, if the hostility is used for constructive ends as in primitive self-defense, then it is a vital reaction to have available, and pathological only when used for immature goals. Thirdly, it is out of place in dealing with most problems of social living, which depends upon the mature capacities for cooperation. Generated from inner, personal, persisting childhood frustrations, misused for immature goals and resorted to in place of mature understanding and cooperation, hostility becomes a disordered adaptive mechanism, a disease of adaptation which is transmitted by contact from parents to children, from generation to generation, and is preventable only by cutting through this process of transmission.

This presents a great challenge to society, one worthy of deep and careful study. Ideally, the best answer is to reduce or eliminate the hostility in the parents themselves. Unfortunately, however, since parents are, after all, only adults who were once children, and we all remain much the children we once were, this is impossible to achieve in any one generation—and to be practical we must settle for the slower pathway of diminishing hostility as much as possible, sublimating the rest, and striving constantly to replace hatred and anger with responsible love and kindness. This is the same as the therapeutic process in the individual, where successful cure means getting him securely on the way to improvement and development.

In this chapter we shall deal with those aspects of hostile behavior that most often occur in the child-parent relationship. In the following chapter we shall deal with the problem of reducing hostility in the adult personality.

Hostility Begins at Home

A key word to good upbringing is *balance*. An excess of attention may be as bad as too little. Too great a demand for growth is as unhealthy as too much babying. The child must be allowed, perhaps encouraged gently, to grow up into a mature interdependent adult, not forced; he must be accepted and respected as an individual who is a member of a group.

Emotional development unfolds from infancy to form the mature patterns of parental and social adaptation. Disturbances in the main lines of development which, as we have seen, are the chief sources of hostility are: 1) persistent and excessive childish dependence; 2) insatiable demands to be loved; 3) extreme demands for prestige motivated by envy and rivalry; 4) a disordered conscience; and, generally, 5) revenge for misguided treatment during childhood.

It is always difficult to give practical advice about emotional problems, especially because they take such very individual form in each person. If it were possible to prescribe for the emotions in the same "miracle-drug" fashion that one can for the purely bodily ills, we might lump together all the following into one antidote for hostility—mature parental love, in which we include understanding and respect for the child's personality. We will amplify what is meant with some general advice, expressed as pragmatically as possible, dealing with disturbances of each of these lines of development.

1. The growth of human beings, as of other animals, from conception to maturity, consists very largely in outgrowing dependence upon the parents. The mature

adult not only can be independent but interdependent. He can let others lean upon him; from being parasitic he becomes parental. If parents overprotect the child, they impede its growth to self-reliance. If they force the child prematurely into independence, they cause an aversion to it. Interference with this development produces an adult who, however powerful physically and intellectually, feels like a child, still craving the protection that he never outgrew.

The underlying need to be dependent usually is in sharp conflict with the desire to be mature, causing an inner sense of insecurity and a reaction of impotent rage. The individual may try to overcompensate through a lust for power. Often these emotional dynamics eventuate in open criminality, even murder. Often too the hostility is directed toward random objects; a readiness to "take it out on the dog" is a most important characteristic. No stable personal relationship or stable society is possible in which individuals, apparently adult, have not sufficiently outgrown their childish dependence.

Almost total dependence during the first five or six years of life is normal, to be expected, and should not be discouraged. In fact, because of other needs, it is generally felt that *some* of what we used to call "spoiling" is healthy during this period. This does not mean, however, that all infantile crying demands should be permitted or rewarded after talking begins, or that the walking child should be kept so close to home and mother that no feelers are put out toward relationships outside the home. Arnold Gesell's book, *Infant and Child in the Culture of Today,* is an excellent study of the physical and social capabilities which parents can expect to find in their sons or daughters at this early age, and can be used as a *guide* though not as a *standard* of activity.

When the child goes to school—at five or six, as the case may be—his independent relationships with the outside world begin. How well he adapts to his larger social world will be reflective of how well he has adapted to family-group life. Trouble signs at this age—including overdependence—should be carefully weighed and the comments of teachers and doctors on how his behavior appears to objective, perhaps even critical, eyes should be examined for guidance on where the child may need help.

In cases of flagrant misbehavior experts should be consulted. There are many excellent child guidance clinics throughout the country which can save the well-intentioned parent of the young child from much later grief. Just a few hours of assistance may be all that is necessary at this age to help the parents understand and correct the trouble at its source, and set them and the children on the right track.

Children who are repeatedly "bad" at this age obviously need help, but overly "good" children may also. The quiet overshy child is often warmly welcomed and admired by his overworked teacher, but excessive compliance may signal lack of outgoingness and potential future difficulties.

The child's independence of his family grows in small ways. His physical skills demand encouragement; but the mother whose fear inhibits bicycle riding or tree climbing is no worse a handicap to the child's independence than the demanding father who flings his child bodily into the lake with the cry of "Sink or swim!" *Balance* between protectiveness and prodding is needed here, just as it is in the child's expanding social life, his maturing emotional life.

With the early teens comes another stock-taking period as once more his growing independence—as against the lack of it—prepares itself for maturity. In this ten-to-thirteen period, the child begins showing natural signals of the breakaway that will eventually lead to the outside world. Because these signals are more gently and quietly expressed than they are apt to be during full adolescence, parents can more readily overlook these or shy away from them, but how criticism of the home, lack of responsibility, failures in affection or lapses in the mores are handled at this stage can be of definite help in stabilizing the child's somewhat later adolescent explorations of the ways of group life, his relationships with the opposite sex and his sometimes reckless attempts at premature adulthood. Basically, though, the core of the child's personality pattern is formed, as we have reiterated, by the time he is between three and six. If this is healthy, through good human relations, he will have no serious problems in adolescence. But, conversely, if his interpersonal relations during these very early years have not been good, problems had best be watched for.

Little real emotional conditioning can be accomplished by parents after the early years, but behavior patterns can still be guided and help obtained, when indicated, in

Hostility Begins at Home

correcting infantile patterns. The wise parent, seeking to avoid future hostility because of the carryover of excessive dependency, will avoid thwarting or overindulging either the early, very real dependency of the infant, and, aid and assist the equally real strivings toward independence, the infantile kernels of which flower in the preteens and the teens.

2. The young child's needs for love are necessarily intense, the parents' love being its only guarantee of food, care and protection. With growth, however, there is an increasing capacity for the enjoyment of loving-giving, culminating at maturity. The child then shifts from the receiving end, loved as a baby, to the giving end, the parent who puts out responsible love and meets the child's all but inexhaustible needs. This same enjoyment of giving as a parent carries over from the emotional life to the individual's social and economic life.

Deprivation and overindulgence are two of the common errors of upbringing which disturb the normal development of the need for love. As has been said earlier, if the emotional diet in early childhood is too rich or too poor, then the appetite for love in later life is distorted. True love is a genuine interest in the child's well-being, *for its own sake*, as well as a respect for his emotional individuality, for which spoiling, overattention, demonstrativeness are almost as poor substitutes as lack of love.

Too great a residue of infantile desires for love cannot be gratified in adult life; it often forms a source of constant frustration leading to irritability, to a sense of hopelessness and depression, to all sorts of neurotic symptoms, including dangerous rage.

It sometimes seems quite difficult to welcome a child into this world with real warmth. He brings with him so many problems—financial worries, caretaking chores, housekeeping upheavals; but the chief, most vital problem is the strain he puts on those areas of emotional immaturity in each parent and the parents' relationship to each other. If we can face the fact, however, that the child himself is not to blame for this stress, but rather our own weaknesses, we are setting our feet upon the right path. True love for a child can only come from those capable of loving-giving. Certainly every child should be a wanted child. The unwanted child is all but foredoomed. If there is a large percentage of unwanted children in a population, then it in all probability accounts for much of the social trouble in that society.

There is probably no one without some capacity for mature love. The problem facing most of us is not total lack, but rather greater development of what we have. Self-control, consistent giving of oneself, patience, affection, understanding, respect—all these help to develop a mature ability to love a child *for himself*. The parent-child relationship is one in which it is true that the more you give, the more you get.

Consider the parent who is quite capable of loving the infant, but who shies away from the independence of the brash thirteen-year-old. Love to be love must be as steady as the North Star, encompassing both the irksome two-o'clock feedings of the baby and the back-talk of the adolescent testing his powers. As Shakespeare put it: "Love is not love that alters when it alterations finds."

3. A third powerful source of irrational hostility is found in an inordinate desire for prestige.

Self-love is, within normal limits, an expression of self-preservation. The very life of a small child depends upon its being highly valued by the parents. But for the adult parent a genuine, unselfish interest in his child, in others and in responsible, productive accomplishment should be more enjoyable than the egocentric satisfactions natural to the child. The child's self-centeredness remains to some degree in the mature adult, but the proportion is changed; no longer are the desire for personal prestige, rivalry and envy major motivations.

Balance again is our key word because of the two most common errors in upbringing which cause excessive drives for prestige and rivalry: favoritism and rejection. If the child's prestige need is not properly handled, then his infantile values of success may persist throughout adult life and he may become the kind of a man of whom Napoleon cynically said, "Men will go through Hell itself for a bit of ribbon." Again and again one observes how little of the interest of an adult lies in the task in hand, and how much it is devoted to using the situation for his vanity. If a child is made to feel that he is the lord of the household or if one parent sides with him consistently against the other, or if the parents expect him to fulfill their own ambitions, then he is prone to be fixed in a power pattern and feel in adult life that he must be the best, the preferred one. His own status will be all that matters and every other person will be to him primarily a hated rival, or a means to prestige. On the other hand, the child who is rejected and not sufficiently valued is likely to carry throughout life a sense of inferiority, an injury to his self-regard, and in vain efforts to heal it, he too will fail to outgrow egotism as a primary motivation. He is foredoomed to frustration and therefore rage and hate, for all competitors can never be vanquished, his childish egotism can never be sated.

This is not to mean that there is anything wrong with healthy ambition, competition and success, provided it is the reflection of self-reliant, friendly, responsible doing, producing, building. It is only when it is mistranslated into egotism, hostile personal rivalry and a childish battle for personal status that it becomes dangerous. This distinction is difficult to make today. The welfare of a society depends upon how much its members contribute, but our current standards of material success are based in great part on how much the members can take out.

The projection of parental ambitions onto the child is a common source of drives for power and prestige in the adult. When a parent compels a child toward the kind of success he or she once dreamed of, this pressure in itself usually creates a source of hostility, as rebellion and protest, as hate of rivals or from frustration of these ingrained compulsive strivings.

4. A fourth common source of irrational hostility is friction between the individual and his conscience. The conscience should be the internalized result of gradual, reasonable socialization, balancing individual desire with the good of others and of society as a whole. But how often is the adult conscience little more than the imago of a depriving or overprotecting or threatening mother

Hostility Begins at Home 173

or a father whose attitudes, feelings and treatment (psychologically or physically) have created feelings that impair rather than help development and that are permanent.

Physically harsh treatment is rarely anything more than the parents' own fears and hostilities being vented upon the helpless. "I'll teach you to hit people," cries the parent in white heat, hitting out at the child. But what a lesson in hostility this turns into! Teaching is accomplished best by example, not precept, and the example here is an enraged adult venting physical violence, a model the child is quite sure to follow. It is pretty certain that if the child were properly reared, the occasions for punishment would not occur.

Emotionally harsh treatment is less obvious but equally or more destructive to personality. The inculcation of too high ideals in childhood dooms the adult to incessant, hopeless striving to achieve the unrealizable. "A man's reach should exceed his grasp"—yes, but not by too much. The piling up in the child of guilt and shame, by the attitudes of the parents, can burden the child for life. The discrepancies between behavior and conscience or the existence of an immature conscience usually form a chronic source of hostility.

The difficulties of the toddler may be those of an experimenter. The selfishness of the young adolescent may be a stage of growth. The sex interest of the growing youth is not necessarily wickedness but preparation for parenthood. *A pura omnia pures*—to the pure all things are pure. There is one central point: *If the child has had good human relationships until the ages of six or seven, the core is sound, and he will move successfully through later stages of development. The later problems regularly have their origin in the earliest years.*

Try to see the adult growing in the child; try to seek a balance in the ideals set before him. If training is forced upon him too early, too harshly or too constantly, his spirit can be crushed; if too late, too leniently or too little, he may become impulse-ridden, lacking secure, automatic controls, and accept immature, even criminal behavior. If training is too inflexible, it may result in an adult so rigid that he will break down for lack of adaptability; if it is inconsistent, it can produce vacillation and confusion. But if the ideals are those of emotional maturity, then the conscience aids a balanced, harmonious development and good interpersonal relations—and life is mostly human relations.

5. A fifth common source of hostility is displaced revenge for any and all sorts of mistreatment, deliberate or unintentional, during childhood. Probably parental hostility to the child is the greatest single source of the lifelong hatreds and readiness to violence which we see so widely in adults; nor is it surprising that the child who comes to hate its own parents should grow up to hate the world. The dense fog of sentiment enshrouding parental love hides much of the stupidity, rejection and abuse to which small children on all levels of society are subjected.

Parents, unknowingly, frequently incite the child's anger and aggressive behavior and then punish it for its reaction. This occurs most commonly because of failure to understand the child's nature and development, by causing demands to be made upon the child beyond its capacities. But a second important cause is the mishandling of the natural rivalries with parents and with brothers and sisters.

Guidance in cooperation is the answer to a fist fight between two young brothers—not another verbal or physical battle between the parent and the children involved. Some thought to the parent's role in the fight should also be given; too often, all unwittingly, the parent's love is the object over which the children are really battling. Children who are predominantly hostile are sending up storm signals of the greatest importance; they must be handled with increased understanding rather than force. For the child he once was lives on in the adult, and so do the images of those who reared him.

To return to the basic question of what a mature parent-child relationship should be, let us now consider some of its general aspects.

As we have repeatedly noted, the key to what is mature as distinct from what is immature lies in the over-all contrast between the parents' feeling and behavior toward the child and the child's feeling and behavior toward the parents. *The child receives, but the parent must give.*

The child, at first, cooperates only to fill his needs. However, through accepting love and through identification with those who give him love, he learns to give it, to grow into his place in the family unit and to enjoy contributing there. All training should be designed to free his potentials for love, cooperation and responsibility. For maturing is a process of growing from the passive-receptive-dependent (PRD) attitudes and feelings of the child toward the parent into the responsible-productive-independent (RPI) ones of the parent to the child.

Parents often ask: "Is it all right to give the child a spanking if it is mild?" Such questions are tangential. *The essential is the good emotional relationship with the child and a good model of behavior for the child.*

It is possible for a father or mother to spank a son or daughter but to do it in such a way that the child feels justly treated. It is also possible for a father or mother never to spank a child, but by tone and manner to create such feelings of shame and guilt in him that his opinion of himself is warped. He thinks of himself as a most inferior creature and this, as we have seen, is a prime source of fear and hostility. When the parents react with vengefulness or nagging, it eventually destroys any possibility of a good relationship and will sow seeds in the child of lasting hate with all its dire consequences in later life, for the child and society. For the child will tend much more to do what the parent does than what the parent says.

In this sense *what* is done is of much less importance than *how* it is done. The parent who is able to keep the child's love and friendship and to provide him with a good model for mature behavior has laid the foundation in that child for the capacity to love and be friendly throughout life. The parent who understands and trusts the course of development, who expects the good rather than the bad, will get it. And the question of spanking will arise rarely, if at all.

Summarizing, the most common abuses in child rearing can be simply grouped along such lines as:

Overprotection	←——→	Underprotection
Overindulgence	←——→	Deprivation, rejection
Excessive domination	←——→	Lack of control
Training too early	←——→	Training too late
Training too fast	←——→	Training too slow
Rigidity and insistence	←——→	Inconsistency
Too high standards	←——→	Inadequate standards
Overvaluation, excessive adoration	←——→	Underevaluation, depreciation
Excessive physical fondling	←——→	Insufficient demonstrativeness

and so on

Often these errors in child rearing are expressions of an undercurrent of parental hostility toward the child, conscious or unconscious; but often they result from ignorance, circumstances, following bad advice, even in the best-meaning and most devoted of parents. Some result from vogues. An example is the behavioristic clock-feeding schedules of not so many years ago, with the child, in psychologically aseptic isolation, left alone to cry his heart out until the appointed hour for feeding, with a concession to nature of just one-half hour per day for holding by the mother.

So long as the parents have genuine good feeling for the infant and its welfare and respect for it as a person, there is a responsive core of healthy good feeling in the infant which provides him with the underlying capacity for good relationships with himself and others. The child responds to love and confidence with love and confidence and, through identification, takes over these feelings and attitudes, modeling himself upon those who care for him. This is his great safeguard—and the parents'—against too extreme warpings of development and emotional disorders.

Love is the indispensable essence. Everyone needs love enormously and desperately. We cannot go after it, therefore, for ourselves, directly as in childhood, without realizing that if we are to get it, others must give it. Love means an unselfish interest in the loved one, for that one's own sake alone, for no ulterior motive. The reward to the parent comes not from exploiting the child in some way during childhood or later, nor from molding it to his or her own wishes. It comes only from the satisfaction of seeing the child develop and live out its life as a fine, healthy, truly mature adult.

The list of common abuses given above is a sample of what interferes with children's growing up into adults who are free to love—spouse, children, friends, fellow man. This interference, by warping the development, generates the hostility which comes to expression as disease and evil. *This little list presents the basic cause of mental and emotional and many other diseases, crime, war and human misery as they are transmitted from generation to generation. Here stands the prime target for prevention.*

There is much detailed information on how to treat children, but the basic principles which confront the parent are relatively brief and simple.

(1) The proper rearing of the child is the first responsibility of marriage. A good relationship with one's

Hostility Begins at Home

husband or wife is an essential to this and this involves the choosing of a proper mate.

(2) The child is not clay to mold but an expression of the forces of nature. His inner biological wisdom has developed over millions of years, and to tamper with it or to go against it can produce only tragedy; like a flower or a tree that needs physical warmth and security he needs to be given the proper conditions of emotional warmth and security to grow and fulfill his own nature. This principle of cultivation might be called, following Harry Lee, *"intelligent neglect." Love them and leave them alone.*

(3) The *golden mean* of balance is a secure guide; problem children come from problem parents and situations.

(4) The necessary training and socializing should be gradual, gentle, consistent over long periods and relying on the *inevitability of gradualness*. Patience, reason and example are to be used, not precept and punishment.

(5) Awareness is essential of the nature of the child's inevitable demands and his intense competition in relation to brothers and sisters and parents; and he is to be helped to handle this and the hostilities involved through tolerance, understanding and free, open discussion. The power of *sympathetic understanding* can hardly be overestimated in building up and keeping a thoroughly good relationship.

(6) The child in his feelings, whatever his behavior, does as the parent does, will feel as the parent feels, far more than as the parent says and does. So the effort is to be made to *give him a proper, mature model* for the

identifications and imagos which will precondition his feelings toward himself and others for the rest of his life.

(7) The *Golden Rule* underlies all relationships including the parent-child relationship. *Do unto others as you would have them do unto you.*

The existence of the home depends upon each member's capacity to love the others and work for and contribute to their welfare. The existence of society depends upon the same feelings and behavior. To enjoy a *value given for a value received* is the law of the family and of society. Kill and grab is the law of the jungle. Any animal can act on the law of the jungle. So can a child, small and weak as he is. It takes a mature human being to act on the law of human family and social living. To repeat, maturity and greatness lie in what we contribute to society, not in what we take out of it.

10 *Fighting the Devil and Seeking the Grail*

ALTHOUGH HOSTILITY is a widespread and malignant disease which underlies many serious social and personal problems, there are powerful curative forces on the side of mankind in efforts to deal with this malady. The problem has two aspects and can be attacked simultaneously in two ways. As Ernest Southard put it: "One can fight the devil or seek the grail." One can attack the devil, "hostility," just as one attacks any other disease by bringing modern science to bear upon it and then making use of the knowledge gained, and at the same time, one can find the way through healthy biological development toward mature interdependence and loving cooperation.

The drives of the organism provide a biological basis for behavior which is constructive for the individual and the species. Ethics, good will, healthy family life—these are not artificial ideals foisted upon us by the necessities of civilization. On the contrary, they are expressions of our basic mature nature. They are the results of adult strength, even as hostility signifies frustration and weakness. Such constructive personal and social forces are strengthened by a tendency toward the evolution of higher forms. We know that phylogenetically there has been progress up the scale from peck orders to true leadership. Civilization itself and what we broadly call "mental development" or "culture" can be seen as part of the evolutionary process, and this process is an aid to the sublimation and control, and, we hope, resolution and outgrowing of man's hostilities. Increasing clinical and experimental evidence that the thrust toward maturity and cooperation can overcome the more primitive fight-flight reflex bears this out. The problem thus appears to be one of education and social engineering—how to accomplish on a world-wide scale what is already being done by proper therapeutic psychoanalytic treatment for individuals.

We have seen how faulty early conditioning produces lifelong deformities of personality which, in turn, generate hostility. But conditioning is something controllable. This has been proved with animals. In a recent experiment with hostility at Tulane University, a cat and a rat need each other in order to push two buttons simultaneously and so raise a partition and get food. They therefore peaceably eat together and establish a close relationship. Whoever has had both dogs and cats as pets knows how quickly they become intimate friends, curl up to sleep together, and suckle each other's young (at least the female dogs suckle the kittens).

On a human emotional level, reconditioning is seen daily in psychoanalytic practice. A neurosis is essentially a persisting disturbed childhood emotional relationship to the parents (and perhaps siblings). It is essentially a

Fighting the Devil and Seeking the Grail 183

repetition and continuation of this relationship, more or less internalized as an interrelationship between the superego and the rest of the personality, and more or less transferred to other persons. The patient also "transfers" this relationship to his analyst, each session providing the doctor with a sort of laboratory sample of the patient's relations to other persons, a sample of his key imagos and reaction patterns. The therapeutic task, then, is to correct these imagos and patterns and thus reopen emotional growth. It is always amazing to see afresh in every person these early relationships repeating:

Mother was so possessive I fear any close relationship lest I be dominated to the extent of losing my independence and friends, just as happened with her. . . . Father was so rejecting that I shun any attachment fearing rebuff. . . . Younger brother was so competitive and took my toys that I feel sure every younger person is a similar threat and is after my possessions, friends, position. . . . Both parents were so unreservedly loving that I feel certain that everyone loves me.

There is an old saw that, in analysis, the patient gives the analyst his superego, the analyst overhauls it and then returns it to him. More concretely, the analyst must *decondition* and *recondition* the patient. Freud called this "after-education," Franz Alexander called it "corrective emotional experience." In accomplishing this one analyzes accurately and thoroughly (1) the imagos that the patient carries; (2) his main emotional relationships to them from his superego and his id (feeling rejected or loved, guilty or ashamed, hostile or beaten down); and (3) the patient's concept of himself in this picture. The old conflictful parental superego figures must be replaced by a new superego which is a tolerant, understanding, supportive, mature one. Progress toward cure is achieved by exposing the pattern of infantile motivations to the patient's highest powers—to his ego—his reason, reality sense, experience, judgment, and by showing what drives are mature, so that he can learn from experience, and through it, outgrow the infantile in favor of the mature.

In the process the analyst comes to replace the authority of the parents. Hence his power, and hence the vital importance of his own personality, his own attitudes, his own clarity, his own maturity, and his own understanding and handling of hostilities. The tendency of the analysand, the person being analyzed, to put himself in the position of a little submissive, dependent child toward the analyst, as he once was toward his parents, is unconscious and automatic. The analyst cannot prevent it, but it is his great responsibility to correct and reduce it in favor of the patient's independence and maturity. Hence the need for the analyst to be "well analyzed" (which should mean "mature") himself.

As the analyst succeeds in altering these disordered childlike feelings, the patient reduces the image of himself as an insecure, guilty child in a world of controlling adults, ceases putting himself emotionally in such a position toward others and comes to see himself *as he is* through the eyes of the analyst, as a person with mature powers for work and love and the capacity to enjoy them in a mature fashion.

Here is a typical example of how this pattern of change occurs: The patient, a man of thirty-two, had been

Fighting the Devil and Seeking the Grail 185

reared by his mother, a strong-willed woman, who hated her husband, his father. Soon after birth, his parents were divorced and as the boy grew up he was told repeatedly what a despicable man his father was. He was forbidden to see him. So thoroughly did his mother drum into him a feeling of depreciation toward his father that he acted out a similar pattern in all his adult relationships; he was only capable of having one friend at a time, corresponding to his mother.

He had fallen in love when he came for treatment and wanted to get married, but he was at once fearful of telling the young woman he was seeing me—and fearful of telling me he was engaged. He simply could not believe that both his friends would not be angry at his having another close relationship and would not take it as a gross and unpardonable disloyalty.

Whatever the improper childhood conditioning, the analyst must make repeatedly clear to the patient the distinction between the reactions formed during early childhood and the present reality. He must constantly confront the patient with his tendency to react to the treatment situation, to others and to himself in terms of this early conditioning and these imagos. He must show that what was logical, appropriate behavior when the patient was a child and helpless before those in charge of him may be unrealistic and unworkable in the present. Only in this way can the patient learn to see himself in his adult make-up, with his mature powers and the capacity for pleasure in exercising them. Only in this way can he learn to see others as they are in reality.

As this young man's problem was revealed he could

finally accept the fact that his analyst sincerely wished him to be happy and was pleased about his love of another rather than taking it as a rejection. A weight was lifted from him—the weight of the possessive, maternal domination to which he had been conditioned. His development was reopened, his capacity for love, responsibility, interest was released and he was at least on the way to becoming a good and loving husband, father and citizen.

Analysis frees the ego from the tyranny of fixed, automatic, unconscious, infantile patterns. Insight, understanding these patterns, is the first step in this re-education, and continues as an essential. But insight alone is usually not sufficient. The central technic for correcting the personality fault is "transference," the repetition of childhood patterns to the analyst. The infantile is "analyzed out" and the mature is freed, so that emotional growth can take place through life experience.

The means of treatment followed by the analyst suggest the growth patterns to be adopted by the generally healthy in seeking emotional maturity and the handling of their hostilities. More than a purely intellectual comprehension of the goals sought and the hazards to be overcome must be achieved by the individual, however, if growth is to occur, for some feeling-insight must accompany the mental processes if they are truly to be effective.

Insight and growth can occur outside of therapy, of course. In meeting demanding situations people often learn and mature. This can be one of the compensations of illness and of other forms of pain and suffering, so often extolled as necessary for the artist.

Development also occurs with religious experiences. Although, as we have noted, religion and psychiatry use different idioms, the concerns of psychiatry and religion are the same, and the emotional experience of insight in both fields is related.

The question remains, however: Is it possible for man to rechannel intellectually, for himself, by himself, the unconscious impulses? It would seem that the answer is no—that what is *unconscious* in each individual cannot be raised to the conscious level solely by one's own deliberate efforts. But before this is taken to mean that it is futile to think a man can attempt new growth alone, let us also note that the intellect can probably aid development. It is possible, therefore, that any man or woman seeking greater strength, higher goals, a deeper capacity for mature love, might find help in consistently educating himself toward these goals and in holding within himself at all times a vision of the ideal. He may then be better prepared to benefit from insight, should it occur; for he will know what to look for in himself and be in a better position to learn from life and science and to develop his mature powers.

In what ways and to what extent different persons can help themselves is as yet not explored scientifically. A severe warping of the personality will never, in all likelihood, be corrected by reading a book. Nevertheless we can realistically hope and expect that much will be gained as people come to recognize the roots of emotional disorders and hence of social disorders, as they come to appreciate what maturity consists of and how indispensable it is for satisfying living, and as they grasp and learn to apply the essential principles of child rearing.

And we can anticipate a happier world as this knowledge is clarified and disseminated and gradually finds a place in our ideology.

Elsewhere we have taken up some of these intellectual aids in our approaches to religion, politics and social problems. Other pragmatic help is to be found in recognizing behavior patterns, in understanding the fundamentals of mature living and in the handling of day-to-day problems.

One of these problems and a general and pressing one is that of achieving a truly *balanced* way of life—a life in harmony with both the progressive and regressive forces, in which the give and the get are in equilibrium. The meaning and implications of such a mode of life are so significant for enjoyment and the reduction of hostility that they are worth looking at closely.

The logic of a balanced life derives from our knowledge, incomplete though it is at present, of the two opposing directions taken in everyone by his or her motivational forces. Biologically, the "progressive" forces impel the organism toward mature, productive, responsible, interdependent efforts, making a happy family and a happy society. But the forces grouped as "regressive" urge the organism to relinquish such productive, creative, working effort, and return to the more passive-receptive-dependence state of foetal life, infancy and childhood.

Fighting the Devil and Seeking the Grail 189

Like chemical anabolism and catabolism, both tendencies are essential to life. Probably no organism of the animal species has been found which can exist in maturity without some independent effort; even forms so completely parasitic that they neither have nor need mouths to nourish them, nevertheless must expend some nonegocentric energy for reproduction to continue their species. In the higher forms, the centrifugal output for the sake of mate, young and social order is usually quite evident. But conversely, all energy output and no re-creation of energy is inconsistent with living. Rest, eating, sleeping, play and the like are *necessary* self-indulgences, and forms of normal essential regression seen throughout the animal kingdom.

For thinking, modern man the art of life has become largely the art of getting these two opposing forces into balance.

This balance involves not only going through the motions of adequate amounts of work and play, but also genuine, deep enjoyment of both these progressive and regressive activities.

While, socially speaking, we instinctively distrust either extreme—the playboy or the loafer at one end, the harried, compulsive slave-driver at the other, there are many reasons why modern man finds the balanced life difficult to achieve. Even what should be sport or play often becomes respected only as work and people must frequently apologize for balancing duty with adequate recreation.

Of course, much of the reason why individuals get trapped in this sort of an attitude stems from inner conflicts. But too many people who are neither neurotic nor conditioned to such patterns also fail to adopt the balanced life simply because they do not recognize its value in mature development and healthy living, and too greatly yield to or too much escape from the constant pressures of modern life.

We have all known people who when they worked longed for relaxation—and when they relaxed, felt they should be working. These people seem to have to force themselves to work and force themselves to play. Each tendency, the progressive and the regressive, drives head-on against the other; the two are never separated so that they can establish a balance and rhythm. Such people can enjoy neither work nor play; they should *enjoy both*.

Sometimes a partly healthy reaction of shame and self-defense against an overindulgent childhood drives a man or woman into compulsive working. Frequently guilt and the need for self-punishment may be the unconscious motivation for too much or too little work. But very common causes are simply our present emphasis on the prestige that goes hand in hand with getting—especially the getting of money. The virtues of healthy ambition are often lost in the excesses. How frequently the sleepless struggle for "happiness" mistranslated into dollar terms brings only suffering, breakdown, a broken home, ulcers, coronary thrombosis and high blood pressure.

For nature will not be outsmarted. We are born to a certain mold and our development follows nature's pattern; we age and mature according to her laws. The only happiness and power lie in understanding and going along with the forces which shape and control us and in

Fighting the Devil and Seeking the Grail 191

whose inexorable grip we are. Vanity and pride are ludicrous in the face of the realities of biology and of the universe, the underlying forces of which made us and use us for their expression. To obstruct their ability to help us make use of our mature powers to love sexually, to win a happy home and to love socially and make a harmonious society, is inevitably to pay the price in emotional disorders and their consequences. Such basic biology, it would seem, should be as fundamental in our schools as the three R's.

All human adults are children for a very long time. During this time they learn the pleasures of being loved, supported, taken care of, valued, rewarded and the pain of being regimented, pushed and possessed. Only the fortunate reach an emotionally mature orientation with its balance of give and get, its balance of work and play.

But to enjoy being a "grown-up," to find any peace, one must shift his emphasis from childish values to the parental goals of contributing to society through work, to his friends, through interest and devotion, and to his own growth, through rest and re-creation of his energies. A successful, effective, mature life is one of balance between the progressive mature motivations and the regressive infantile ones. With both in order and balance the person can *enjoy both.*

11 *Looking Forward*

The means of treatment suggest the means of prevention. The analyst sees the fight-flight reaction as it operates in all sorts of emotional suffering. He knows that it is intrinsic to probably every symptom of disturbed motivation, and that it cannot be reduced without understanding and love.

Analytic therapy, which above all involves mature interest in another, is itself a sublimated form of love in the broad sense of the term. The analysand must be seen as a friend to be understood and helped, never used as a source for praise or anything else for the analyst except as a mature value for a value. Analytic therapy means not reacting to the patient's childish demands and hostilities, but enduring them with tolerance and friendliness in order to understand, analyze and resolve them. It is also, as we have noted previously, a form of emotional education or, more precisely, emotional re-education. Analysis reveals and seeks to correct the errors in the patient's upbringing, the errors which disturbed his development and thereby produced his feelings of inferiority and frustration and other sources of his hostility.

Thus knowledge has accumulated of the proper course of human development, of what constitutes maturity and of the inevitable problems which, with guidance, the child must solve if he is to grow up adequately and to enjoy living out his life in the full flowering of his mature, constructive powers, with all that this means to himself, his family, his nation, his species.

To this basic knowledge, all of the psychological, biological and social sciences can contribute. Because of the overlapping of the various fields, interdisciplinary teams should be especially effective. Much more should be done than at present. Existing scientific societies might form sections for the investigation of how to grow better human beings. At present more is done to study and achieve the growth of hogs and cattle than of men. A special society might well be formed to bring together all scientists who share this interest, like the national societies for cancer or heart disease. Promising young men and women might be recruited from our educational system as researchers in this field. Ideally, a "Manhattan District Project" should be organized for the study of human development and for combating its chief obstruction, man's hostility to man. The growing body of knowledge could then be made constructively effective through school, church and state, and through other organizations, as well as through individuals such as writers, dramatists and artists.

Through the physical scientists we are developing an amazing technology of production, distribution, communication, and transportation. We can expect that in time the social scientists—the economists, political scientists, sociologists and others—will help us to improvements in social organization. The power of circumstances is obvious. The stresses, insecurities, anxieties, complexities, with which adults struggle to maintain themselves and their families and establish a place in society influence everyone, how he lives, what strains he sustains, what breakdowns he suffers in his body and in his mind. But full solution cannot come from increasing improvements in social organization alone, for at the bottom, the most perfect organization consists of people and will not operate maturely unless the individual men and women who constitute it are sufficiently mature. Organization, in fact, should be directed toward achieving the proper development of children and the proper conditions of life for mature adults. The epiorganism always reflects the characteristics of the unit organisms which compose it; our bodies have the earmarks of their cells; our society, of its individuals.

Our times are marked by a great paradox: man tends to use his enormously increased power over nature much less for his good than for his destruction. Therefore his realization of the dream of science to tap the power of the atom has brought him, not rejoicing over new wealth and new security, but fear of total destruction.

This paradox springs from the fact that each individual in our society is activated by strong asocial or antisocial motivations as well as by social ones. Survival has become a matter of understanding these two sets of impulses in order to aid the constructive, pro-human, and reduce the destructive, anti-human motivations—to increase what is *for* human life and decrease what is *against* it.

Looking Forward

The fundamentals of human relationships, biologically based as they are, do not change perceptibly over the centuries and millennia. The problems of production, distribution and social organization are not insuperable for the human intellect which has succeeded in exploring the atom and interstellar space. These problems plague us, not because they are technically insoluble, but because our own emotions get in the way. If a tiny fraction of what is spent on armaments were spent on studying human destructiveness and human constructiveness, then just as science has reduced for us the terrors of inanimate nature and even of disease, it might show us how to reduce the terrors of that threatening disease within man himself, his hostility to his fellows.

Moses forbade violence. Jesus taught the need for love. Jefferson sought freedom of the mind through principles, politics and education. Freud reached the same conclusions through the paths of science and showed the obstacles to accomplishing these ends. Now it is for us, the ordinary people, to understand and work toward the removal of the obstacles and the achievement of the goal, be it called "salvation" by religion, "democracy" by government, or "emotional maturity" by psychiatry. This is the grail. The devil is the incarnation of evil, and evil is disordered infantile impulses, chief of all man's hostility to man. Hostility can be attacked at its roots: in the rearing of the child and the re-education of the adult. It can be banished as smallpox and typhoid have been banished in this country. Then we shall realize the dream of producing mature, constructive men and women so that there may be many of them among us. The ancient war of good against evil, of love against hate, of God against Devil, of democracy against tyranny, is also the war of the mature and loving people against the infantile and hostile people. In this struggle lies humanity's most thrilling challenge; in the outcome, the hope of a desperate world.

Why should this fight reaction, this hostility, be so intensely and constantly aroused in some individuals and not in others? There may be rational external reasons for this or irrational internal ones. But examining a series of individuals in all walks of life, one is struck by the fact, as noted earlier, that there is relatively little correlation between the person's situation in life and how antagonistic and dangerous he is.

The same is true for social groups and nations today. When two ancient savage tribes were dependent upon the same herd of animals for food, it was perhaps rational for one to destroy the other in order to preserve itself. Perhaps it can be said that it is still rational to attack when one is attacked; but the original attack itself may be irrational. Certainly when the proverbial "visitor from Mars" sees the whole world divided into armed camps knowing that war brings not more food but famine, not security but death and destruction—whereas even moderate cooperation would result in rising standards of living for all—then, how can he help but perceive a basic irrationality? War is not reasonable but unreasonable; irrationality is the true source of war.

And if individual after individual is examined for the irrational sources of his hostilities, these disordered infantile patterns are almost invariably found in abundance.

Looking Forward

The conclusion is inevitable: man's inhumanity to man springs almost entirely from *irrational* sources so contrary to nature that direct violence now appears as a holdover, like the appendix, but infinitely more dangerous.

For the individual today cannot meet his difficulties by physical attack. He gets on by proper social behavior: cooperation, responsibility, productivity and interdependence. The fight-flight reaction as a method for solving the complex problems of modern social adjustment is like trying to repair a fine watch with a hammer. Democracy fails when the forum breaks down and violence is used.

Fortunately man's readiness to hostility and violence against others, while part of his automatic fight-flight reaction, cannot be dismissed as a fixed quantity, with which he is born and which cannot be changed. Hostility, like sex, is a basic biologic force which varies from person to person in intensity, indulgence and forms of expression. Many persons have very little sexual feeling; others so much that they suffer acutely. Not only the object but the aim and form of the sexual activity vary as widely as human imagination; so does the content—for some, the sexual relationship expresses love and affection, for others it is an attack which can lead to rape and lust-murder. So, too, there is a tremendous difference in the amount and expression of hostility in the extreme Mr. Milquetoast who cannot even kill a fly and in a homicidal criminal. Happily, in every person who is successfully treated psychoanalytically, the underlying irritations which cause his hostility are diminished, as is the hostility itself. While we see then that there is enormous variation from person to person in the intensity of hostile feelings, in how freely and in what ways he vents them in actions, we also see how responsive he can be to cure, how eager to learn to love and mature.

Nor is it hard to distinguish the mature, constructive and reasonable motives in oneself and others from the disordered infantile, egocentric, hostile ones. People should understand the tremendous importance of this for their personal lives, for their children and for society.

Hostility should be made universally known for what it is, a neurotic symptom, a symptom of weakness and frustration, a primitive method of defense which has become mankind's principal enemy and threatens to destroy him. We should know that Neros are made, not born, that evil and violence have their genesis in the mishandling of the emotions, that they are preventable perversions.

The problem should be tackled by all the related sciences. It should be pursued as widely and energetically as cancer, tuberculosis, infantile paralysis and heart disease combined. Our best brains, with adequate funds, should be mobilized to attack this program on a national scale. Hostility is a mass neurosis or psychosis in the true sense of the term.

What is already known should be disseminated systematically and as widely as possible to improve the upbringing of our children and the lives of our adults. In the long run, our security will not rest with atom bombs but with a population which is strong, realistic and resourceful, through its achievement of emotional maturity. The best available information should be made readily accessible through libraries, mass media, schools and churches, and all those who deal with people and particularly with children. It should reach men and women of all ages, all stages of the life cycle, so that it may take the place it deserves in our ideology. The greatest single effort of the nation and of the world should be devoted to seeing that its children mature emotionally from the moment of conception. This is the basic answer to man's tendency to torture and destroy himself. The practical difficulties *can* be overcome. When they are, peace and brotherhood will be, not sentimental dreams, but practical reality, and man will have saved himself from being a far more spectacular biological failure than the dinosaur.

REFERENCES

(Only immediate references are given. A comprehensive bibliography on Hostility, comprising about 450 references to the technical literature, is not presented here, but publication of it in the near future is anticipated.)

Part One

HUXLEY, JULIAN, "Knowledge, Morality and Destiny," *Psychiatry*, Vol. xlv, No. 2, May, 1951.

ALLEE, W. C., *Co-operation among Animals*. New York, Henry Schuman, 1951.

JENNINGS, H. S., "The Beginnings of Social Behavior in Unicellular Organisms," *Science*, Vol. xcii:539, 1940.

FRISCH, KARL, *Bees, Their Vision, Chemical Senses and Language*. Ithaca, Cornell University Press, 1951.

HASKINS, CARYL, *Of Societies and Men*. New York, Norton, 1953.

SELYE, HANS, *The Physiology and Pathology of Exposure to Stress*. Montreal, Acta, Inc., 1950.

CANNON, WALTER, *Bodily Changes in Pain, Hunger, Fear and Rage*. New York, Appleton, Century, 1928.

SAUL, LEON J., *The Bases of Human Behavior*. Philadelphia, J. B. Lippincott, 1951.

DEJONG, HERMAN H., *Experimental Catatonia*. Baltimore, Williams and Wilkins, 1945.

FREUD, SIGMUND, *A General Introduction to Psychoanalysis*. Garden City, N.Y., Garden City Publishing Co., 1943.

ALEXANDER, FRANZ, *Our Age of Unreason*. Philadelphia, J. B. Lippincott, 1942.

References

The crime statistics are difficult to establish accurately and were gathered from several sources. Most of them are derived from William C. Menninger, "Facts and Statistics of Significance for Psychiatry," *Bulletin*, Menninger Clinic, 12:25, 1948. Other sources include: Rowntree, Leonard, et al., "Mental Health and Personality Disorders in Selective Service Registrants," *J.A.M.A.*, 128:1084-1087, 1945. Bullis, H. Edmund, and O'Malley, Emily E., *Human Relations in the Classroom*, Wilmington, Del. *The Army Almanac*, 1950. *Veterans Administration's Technical Bulletin* TB 10-59, Nov. 30, 1949. FBI Crime Reports, *New York Times*, April 25, 1945.

Part Two

SAUL, LEON J., *Emotional Maturity*. Philadelphia, Lippincott, 1951.

STRECKER, EDWARD, *Their Mothers' Sons*. Philadelphia, Lippincott, 1951.

SUTTIE, IAN D., *The Origins of Love and Hate*. New York, Julian Press, 1952.

ADLER, ALFRED, *The Practice and Theory of Individual Psychology*. New York, Harcourt, Brace, 1924.

FERENCZI, SANDOR, *Stages in the Development of the Sense of Reality*, in *Sex or Psychoanalysis*. New York, Basic Books, 1950.

WOODS, RALPH L., *World of Dreams*, New York, Random House, 1947.

ADORNO, T. W., Frenkel-Brunswick, Else, et al., *The Authoritarian Personality*. New York, Harper and Brothers, 1950.

FREUD, SIGMUND, *Civilization and Its Discontents*. London, Hogarth Press, 1930.

ALLEE, W. C., *Co-operation among Animals*. New York, Henry Schuman, 1951.

FREUD, ANNA, AND BURLINGHAM, DOROTHY, *War and Children*. New York, Medical War Books, 1943.

BENEDICT, RUTH, *Patterns of Culture*. Boston, Houghton Mifflin, 1934.

MEAD, MARGARET, *Male and Female*. New York, William Morrow and Co., 1949.

Part Three

FREUD, SIGMUND, *Totem and Taboo*. New York, Moffat, 1918.

SAUL, LEON J., *Emotional Maturity*. Philadelphia, Lippincott, 1947.

ALEXANDER, FRANZ, *Fundamentals of Psychoanalysis*. New York, Norton, 1948.

FREUD, SIGMUND, *Civilization and Its Discontents*. London, Hogarth Press, 1930.

ZILBOORG, GREGORY, *The Psychology of Criminal Acts and Punishments*. Isaac Ray Lectures, 1954.

COMFORT, ALEX, *Authority and Delinquency in the Modern State*. London, Routledge and Kegal Paul Ltd., 1950.

ALEXANDER, FRANZ, *The Psychoanalysis of the Total Personality*. New York, Nervous and Mental Diseases Publishing Co., 1929.

ALEXANDER, FRANZ, *Psychosomatic Medicine*. New York, Norton, 1950.

ALEXANDER, FRANZ, "The Neurotic Character," *International Journal of Psychoanalysis*, 2:293, 1930.

SZASZ, THOMAS S., "The Role of Hostility in the Pathogenesis of Peptic Ulcer," *Psychosomatic Medicine*, lx, 1947.

SAUL, ET AL., "An Attempt to Quantify Emotional Forces Using Manifest Dreams," *Science*, March 19, 1954.

SAUL, LEON J., "Psychological Settings of Some Attacks of Urticaria," *Psychosomatic Medicine*, iii, No. 4, 1941.

SAUL, LEON J., "Physiological Effects of Emotional Tension," *Personality and Behavior Disorders*, Vol. I. New York, The Ronald Press Co., 1944.

WEISS, EDWARD, AND ENGLISH, O. SPURGEON, *Psychosomatic Medicine*. Philadelphia, Saunders, 1943.

Part Four

FRENCH, T. M., "Social Conflict and Psychic Conflict," *American Journal of Sociology*, 44:922, 1939.

FRENCH, T. M., *The Psychodynamic Problem of Democracy in Civilian Morale*. Boston, Houghton Mifflin, 1942.

SCHAFFNER, BERTRAM, *Fatherland*. New York, Columbia University Press, 1943.

LEVY, DAVID, "The German Anti-Nazis," *American Journal of Orthopsychiatry*, Vol. xvi, 1946.

KLINEBERG, OTTO, "Tensions Affecting International Understanding," Social Service Research Council, *New York Bulletin*, 62, 1950.

FREUD, SIGMUND, *Group Psychology and the Analysis of the Ego*. New York, Liveright, 1949.

FREUD, SIGMUND, "Certain Neurotic Mechanisms in Jealousy, Paranoia and Homosexuality," *Collected Papers*, Vol. II. London, Hogarth Press, 1924.

JONES, ERNEST, *The Life and Work of Sigmund Freud*, Vol. I. New York, Basic Books, 1952.

SELYE, HANS, "The General Adaptation Syndrome, Textbook on Endocrinology," *Acta Endocrinologica*. Montreal, 1949.

KEEPER, N. N., *You Are Greater Than You Know*. Partnership Foundation, 1955.

DOSTOYEVSKY, F., *Short Stories of Dostoyevsky*. New York, Dial Press, 1946.

JONES, RUFUS, *The Faith and Practice of the Quakers*. London, Methuen and Co. Ltd., 1946.

Part Five

FRENCH, T. M., *The Psycho-Dynamic Problem of Democracy and Civilian Morale*. Boston, Houghton Mifflin, 1942.

GESELL, ARNOLD, *Infant and Child in the Culture of Today*. New York, Harper and Brothers, 1943.

SPOCK, BENJAMIN, *Commonsense Book of Child Care*. New York, Duell, Sloan and Pearce, 1946.

WOLF, ANNA, *The Parent's Manual*. New York, Simon and Schuster, 1941.

SOUTHARD, E. E., AND JARRETT, M. C., *The Kingdom of Evils*. New York, Macmillan, 1941.

FREDRICSON, E., "Aggressiveness in Female Mice," *Journal of Comparative and Physiological Psychology*, 45:254-58, 1952.

FREUD, SIGMUND, *Outline of Psychoanalysis*. New York, W. W. Norton, 1950.

ALEXANDER, FRANZ, AND FRENCH, T. M., *Psychoanalytic Therapy*, New York, The Ronald Press, 1942.

FREUD, SIGMUND, "Character Types Met with in Psychoanalytic Work," *Collected Papers*, Vol. IV. London, Hogarth Press, 1924.

Index

Accidents, incidence of, 23
Adaptation, 10
Addiction, 38
Adolescence, 168, 173
Aggression and hostility, 3
Alcoholism
    fight-flight in, 17
    incidence of, 24
Alexander, Franz
    "corrective emotional experience," 37, 183
    Fundamentals of Psychoanalysis, 74
    libido theory, revised, 33
    and "neurotic character," 100
    Our Age of Unreason, 20
    Psychosomatic Medicine, 110
Allee, Warder C., 11, 12, 48
Ambition of parents projected to children, 172
Analytic treatment, *See* Psychoanalytic treatment
Anger, defined, 3
Antisocial behavior, 67
Anxiety
    and fear, 50-53
    from hostility, 51-53, 84, 155

Balance in mature life
    between giving and getting, 188-191
    between progressive and regressive forces, 188-191
    between work and play, 190-191
Bases of Human Behavior, The (by Leon J. Saul), 19
Bible, hostility in, 65
Biological basis
    of culture, 182
    of emotional maturity, 191
    of religion, 141-149
    of social forces, 181

Blood pressure, high
    as reaction against regression, 21
    as reaction to hostility, 111
Burr, Aaron, 74

Cannon, Walter, 13, 14
"Castration anxiety," 159-160
Catatonia, withdrawal in, 17
Child-parent relationship, *See* Childhood conditioning and training
Childhood
    earliest years of, 28
    importance of good human relationship in, 83, 176
    prolonged, 28
Childhood conditioning and training
    in classic neurosis, 106-109
    controllable, 182
    in criminal, 77-78, 82-85
    in criminoid mechanism, 88-89, 93-95
    errors in, 165-166, 169, 171, 177
    forming conscience and superego, 45-47
    importance of, 27-61, 164-180
    inconsistent, 46-47, 174
    influence on criminality, 77-78
    influence on hostility, 66
    influence on political feelings, 121-137
    influence on social characteristics, 57-58
    need for balance in, 165, 168-169, 171
    in "neurotic character," 101-104
    in neurotic criminal, 97-99
    of physical punishment, 173-176
    in primitive cultures, 57-58
    in psychosomatic mechanism, 112-114
    in sublimated hostility, 116-117
    via identification, 94, 175-180
    via object relationships, 94

Index

Childhood emotional pattern
  controllable, reversible, in animals, 182
  persistence into adulthood, 32, 40, 46, 82
  persistence into marriage, 83, 90, 93
  reconditioning humans in psychoanalytic treatment, 182-183
Christ, 140, 147, 195
Civilization and Its Discontents (by Sigmund Freud), 7
Classic neurosis, 68, 104-109
  defined, 104
  hostilodynamics in case of, 105
Clement, 147
Comfort, Alex, 86
Competitiveness, 31, 39-44; See also Rivalry
"Complexity States," 59-61
Compulsion neurosis, hostility in, 20
Compulsion, 155
Conditionability
  of human mind, 28
  use in psychoanalytic treatment, 37
Conscience, 6, 30-31, 45-47
Consciousness, 30
Cooperation, 10, 182
  biological tendency toward, 11
  as survival mechanism, 10-11
Cooperation Among Animals (by Warder C. Allee), 12
Crapsey, Adelaide, 2
Crime, incidence of, 23
Criminal mechanism, 67, 76, 85
  defined, 78-80
  family influences, 98
  fight and flight fused in, 21-22
  hostilodynamics of, 67, 81-85
  motivation, essential for evaluation, 80
  quality of, 79
  quantitative factor, acceptance by ego, 79
  social influences on, 77-78
  sources of, 77
Criminoid mechanism, 67, 85-95
  anti-social quality, 89-90
  defined, 85-86, 93, 95
  guilt absent in, 87-90, 92-93
  hostilodynamics in case of, 88-89, 90-95
  relationship with politics, 87-90
"Culture," influence on hostilities, 182

Delinquency, incidence of, 23
Delusion, 21
Democracy, 122, 195
Demagogue, 87-90, 121
Dependence, 31-36, 107
  balanced with independence, 168
  hostilodynamics in case of, 35-36
  independence, growth to, 165-169
  and needs for love, 36-38
  reduction, in adolescence, 168
  as source of hostility, 35
Depression
  hostility in as suicide, 19
  withdrawal in, 19
Deprivation, 19
Despotism, 123
Displacement of hostility, 85
Divorce, incidence of, 23
Dix, Dorothea Lynd, 115
Dostoyevsky, 146
Dreams
  guilt, 52
  hostility in, 52, 131-133, 135
  of "leftists," 133-135
  projection in, 56, 131-133
  of punishment, 156-158
  regression in, 21
  of "rightists," 133-134
  of snakes as objects of prejudice, 131-133
Drives, basic biological, 30-32
Drugs, 17
"Dual conscience," 87

Education, and social progress, 182
Ego
  control of hostility, 66
  functions, 29-30, 32
  in neurotic criminal, 96
  in psychosis and neurosis, 73
Emotional forces, See Motivation
Emotional growth and development
  in psychoanalytic treatment, 182-186
  with religious experience, 187
Emotional Maturity (by Leon J. Saul), 31
Emotional maturity
  biological basis of, 190-191
  defined, 31-32
  as goal of psychiatry, 195
  goal of psychoanalytic treatment, 182-186
"Enjoy both"
  balance between progressive and regressive forces, 188-191
  give-get balance, 189-191
  inability to, from failures in emotional growth, 190-192
  work and play balance, 188-191
Envy, 31
Evil and hostility, 4
Erotization
  of any emotion, 75
  of hostility, 74
Ethics and morality
  expressions of mature social cooperation, 121
  science and, 140

Index

Failure as hostility to parents, 154
Family development
   child's adaption to dependent role, 32-37
   Oedipal situation, rivalry with parents, 123
   problems in, 122
   sibling rivalry, 122
Fairbairn, 33
Fantasy, form of flight, 15
Favoritism, 171
Fear
   and anxiety and hostility, 50-53
   from hostility, 155
Field, H. E., 59-61
Fight reactions, ease of expression, 23
Fight-flight reaction, 10, 17, 50, 110-111, 155, 182, 192, 197
   essential to survival in primitive situation, 12-14
   fused, 19, 21, 22
   ineffective or destructive in cooperative civilized culture, 14
   physiological responses to, 15
Fixation of basic emotional force, 35
Flight
   actual, 15
   drugs, 17
   fantasy and sublimation, 15
   psychological forms of, 15-22
   "withdrawal states," 17
Freud, Anna, 51
Freud, Sigmund, 20, 44, 146
   Civilization and Its Discontents, 7
   on "classic neurosis," 39
   conversion hysteria, 110
   on death instinct, 7
   on democracy, 123
   on dependence, 33
   on dreams, 156
   General Introduction to Psychoanalysis, 137
   Group Psychology and the Psychoanalysis of the Ego, 122
   on hostility, 7-8, 22, 65
   instinct theory of, 7
   "object interest," 39
   on paranoiac jealousy, 158
   on regression, 22
   and religion, 139-141
   "return of the repressed," 108
   on sexual theory, eros, 7, 48, 139, 140
   on superego development, 47
   treatment, "after education," 37, 183

General Introduction to Psychoanalysis (by Sigmund Freud), 137
Gesell, Arnold, *Infant and Child in the Culture of Today*, 166
Give-get balance, 38, 107, 188
"Good do indirectly what the bad do directly," 150, 154
Government, goal of, 195
Groups, 12
Guilt, 6
   in classic neurosis, 108
   creating need for punishment, 6, 96, 99, 153-160
   from hostile behavior and/or impulse, 154-155
   from hostility, 52-53, 96, 99-108, 103-160
   in neurotic criminal, 99
   from parental training, 46

Hallucinations, regression in, 21
Harvey, William, 6
Hate, and hostility, 4
Healing, 141
Healthy, compared with normal, 87
Hoover, Herbert C., 161
Hostility
   aggression, compared with, 3
   and anxiety, 50-53
   from childhood, 52-58
   in classic neurosis, 68, 104-109
   controlled, 81
   in conversion hysteria, 110
   in criminal mechanism, 67, 81-85
   definition, 3-4
   from disordered superego, 47, 52-53, 153-160, 165
   displaced to other object, 85
   in dreams, 52, 55-57
   ease of expression, 23
   and ego strength in neurosis, 73
   and ego strength in psychosis, 73
   erotization of, 74-75
   from excessive desires for prestige, 39-44, 165, 171
   from excessive needs for love, 36-39, 165-170
   from excessive power drive, 41
   expressed in failure, 154
   expressed through one organ, 110
   expression of, 74
   and fear, 50-53
   from feelings of inferiority, 39-44
   forms taken by, 71-72
   Freud on, 8, 22, 65
   from frustrated dependence, 35, 107, 165-169
   fused with responsibility, 116-117
   fused in sex, 49, 150
   and happiness, 150-160
   history of, 65
   in hypertension, 111
   from id, 102
   importance of, 8
   incidence of, 23-24

Index

manifestations of, 67-69
in masochism, 75
and maturity, 137, 139
motivations of, 71, 80
in "neurotic character," 68, 99-104
in neurotic criminal, 68, 95-99
as neurotic symptom, 8, 27, 61, 108
not inherited, 27
not strength, 5
from parent to child, 177
in peptic ulcer, 112
in political feelings, 121-137
prevention and cure of, 161-180, 195
privately expressed, 68
projected, 47, 52, 55-57
in psychosomatic conditions, 68
quality of, 79
quantitative factors in, 79
from rejection, 171-172
and religious feelings, 137-149
repressed, 81, 107, 150-160
    overcompensation, 115
    producing anxiety, 84, 107
results of, 15-24
in sadism, 75
self-directed as punishment, 153
in sexual rebellion against parents, 150
socially expressed, 68
sources of, 27-61, 66, 165-180, 197
status of, relative to rest of personality, 66-69
sublimated, 69, 81, 114-117
from superego, 102
suppressed, 81
unconscious, 84, 163
as world's greatest problem, 8
Hostilodynamic mechanisms, 65-117; See also Hostility
Hostilodynamics, definition, 69
Human nature, now understood, vii
Human society
    similarities to non-human societies, 11-12
    warfare between groups, 12-13
Hypertension
    hostility in, 111
    as reaction against regression, 21
"Hysterical" behavior, 20

Id, 30, 32, 66
    source of hostility, 102
    source of mature drives, 31
Identification
    child with parent, 45, 94
    with oppressor, 130
    with siblings, 116-117
Imagos, 53
    correction in treatment, 183-186
    from parental training, 45-47
    and prejudices, 55

projection, 55
split, 54
Incidence, 23-24
Independence
. balance with dependence, 168
    basic emotional force, 34, 165-169
    increase in adolescence, 168
Inferiority feelings, 31, 32, 39-44
    from childhood condition, 42-44
    from dependence, 35
    and political feelings, 129
    projected as prejudices, 55
    a source of hostility, 43-44
Injuries to self, 155
Instinct theory, 17
Interdependence, basic emotional force, 34-35
Integration of feelings, 75
Integrative powers, 29
Intelligence, 59
Introjection, 45

Jealousy, 50, 158-159
Jefferson, Thomas, 74, 145, 195
Jesus Christ, 140, 147, 195
Jones, Rufus, *The Faith and Practice of the Quakers*, 147-148

Klineberg, Otto, *Tension Affecting International Understanding*, 121

Lee, Harry, 179
Libido theory, 33
Life cycle, biological force, 9-10
Lincoln, Abraham, 123, 128, 145
Love
    and "abject interest," 39
    capacity for giving increased by psychoanalytic treatment, 139-149
    child's response to, 177-178
    mature, 144-149, 165-180
    maturity and, 141
    needs for, 31-32
        from childhood training, 40
        and dependence, 36, 37, 38
        displaced to other objects, 38
        give-get balance in, 169-170
        source of hostility, 36-39
    and sex, 48-50
    substitutes for, 98
    therapeutic effect of, 101

Macbeth, Lady, 96
Male and Female (by Margaret Mead), 57-58
Marriage
    child rearing, responsibility of, 178
    relation to childhood conditioning, 83, 90, 93-94
    as stress to adult, 106

Index

Masochism, 7, 153
   sexual, 75
Mature love, of parents for children, 170
Maturity, emotional
   defined, 31-32
   love and, 36, 48-50
   and national security, 198
   potential in child, 29
   and religious feelings, 127-149
   responsibility, productivity and independence, 29
   source in id, 31
Mead, Margaret, *Male and Female*, 57-58
Minister, 149
Morality, 121, 139
   science and, 140
Moses, 140, 195
Motivation
   antisocial, 5
   of hostile behavior, 80
   internal, 71, 72
   major mental, 31-61
   progressive, 33
   quantity of childish, 33
   reactive, 71, 72
   regressive, 33
   social, 5
   for survival, 59-61

Narcissism, 137, 171
Needs for love, *See* Love
Neurosis
   definition of, 182
   ego in, compared with psychosis, 73
   incidence of, 24
   regression in, 20
"Neurotic character," 20, 68, 99-104
   case of, 101-104
   childhood pattern of, 101-104
   compared with other reactions, 100
   guilt in, 102
   hostilodynamics of, 68, 99-104
   introduced by Alexander, 100
   "psychopath," 100
Neurotic criminal, 68, 95-99
   childhood conditioning, 97-99
   conscience in
      conscious, 96
      unconscious, 97
   and "fate neurosis," 97
   hostilodynamics in case of, 95-99
Nightmares, 52, *See also* Dreams
Normal, compared with healthy, 87
Nuclear energy, 5

Oedipal relationship, 121-124
   influence on political feelings, 121-127
O'Sheel, Shaemas, 63
Overcompensation, 115, 117

Overindulgence, 169
Overprotection in childhood, results of, 166
   withdrawal in adults, 18-19

Paranoid jealousy, 158-159
Parent-Child relationship; *See* Childhood conditioning and training
   errors in, summary, 177
   mature parental love in, 165-180
   parental responsibility in, 178-180
   parental hostility to child, 177
Parenthood, as stress, 106, 170
Passive-receptive-dependent attitude (PRD), 175
Paul, 142
Peptic ulcer
   flight in, 21
   hostilodynamics in case of, 112-114
Persecution, ideas of, 155
Personality
   formed before six, 168
   influenced by childhood conditioning, 45-47
   structure, 29-32
Perversion, 20
Phobias, 20
   and hostility, 51-53
Physical punishment, by parents, 173-176
Plasticity of human mind, *See* Conditionability
Plato, 154
Poe, Edgar Allan, 25
Political feelings
   from childhood pattern, 121
   of conditioning and training, 121-137
   from envy and competition, 127-128
   from feeling of inferiority in childhood, 129
   "leftism," 133-135
   from Oedipal relationship, 123-124
   from parental rejection, 126
   "rightism," 133-135
   from sibling rivalry, 122-123
Power, drive for, 41, 44
   forms of, 41
   hostility in, 41, 43-44, 172
   from inferiority feelings, 42
   from parental ambition, 171-172
Prejudice, 132, 135
   from projection, 55, 57
Prestige, excessive desires for
   from parental domination, 39-40
   from parental favoritism or rejection, 171
   from parental overemphasis on competition, 40-41
   from projection of parental ambitions, 172
   as source of hostility, 39
Preventive psychiatry, 192

Index

Progressive emotional forces, 33, 188
  balanced with regressive, 188
  from parental ambition, 172
Projection, of hostile impulses, 47, 52
Provocation from need for punishment, 102
Psychoanalysis
  and morality, 139-140
  and religious feelings, 137-149
Psychoanalytic treatment, 31, 35, 38, 45, 135-137, 164, 182-191
  as after-education, 37, 182-187
  correction of distorted imagos, 183-186
  as corrective emotional experience, 3, 37, 114
  ego strengthened, 184-186
  goal identical to religion, 139-149
  hostility, reduced in, 114
  indications for, 154
  insight in, 89, 114, 185, 186
  love capacity increased, 139-149
  mature love in, 192
  of peptic ulcer, 113-114
  reconditioning in, 182-183
  reopens emotional growth, 183a, 186, 192
  superego analyzed in, 183-184
  transference in, 183-186
Psychoanalyst, 149, 182
  replaces parents in psychoanalytic treatment, 183
Psychodynamics, *See* Hostilodynamics
Psychology of Criminal Acts (by Gregory Zilboorg), 75
"Psychopath," 100
Psychosis
  ego in, 73
  incidence of, 24
  regression in, 21
Psychosomatic condition
  flight in, 21
  hostility in, 109-114
Psychosomatic mechanism, 68, 109-114
  hostility in, 109-114
  mechanism of symptom formation, 110-114
  symbolization, 110
Punishment
  needs for, 6
  in classic neurosis, 108
  determined by source of hostility, 154
  in dreams, 156, 158
  forms of, 155
  in neurotic character, 102
  in neurotic criminal, 96, 99
  physical, by parents, 173-176
"Punishment fits the source" of hostility, 102, 109, 154, 160
  determined by pattern of childhood conditioning, 155-159

Reality, sense of, 32, 53
  distorted by parental training, 53-61
  disturbed by projection, 53
  improved by psychoanalytic treatment, 185
Reconditioning, emotional, in psychoanalytic treatment, 182
Regression
  always as cause, result, or concomitant of hostility, 22
  essential component of all psychopathology, 20, 33-34
  physical withdrawal in, 17
  psychological, 19
  studied first by Freud, 22
Regressive forces, 33
  balanced with progressive forces, 188
  interplay with progressive force, 33
  element in all psychopathology, 20, 33-34
Rejection, 171
Religion, 139, 187
  biological nature of, 141-149
  goal of, 195
  psychoanalysis and, 140-149
Religious feeling
  and ability to love, 139-149
  and hostility, 137-149
  and humility, 146
  and maturity, 137-149
Repression, 81, 150
  "return of the repressed," 154
Responsibility
  fused with hostility, 116-117
  RPI (Responsibility-productivity-independent attitude), 29, 176
Revenge, 81
Richard III, 44
Rivalry, 40
  child with parents, 122
  influence on views of social equality, 123
  sibling, 122-123

Sadism, 75
"Salvation," goal of religion, 147, 195
Saul, Leon J.
  Bases of Human Behavior, The, 19
  Emotional Maturity, 21
School, 165
Sensuality, 48
Sex, 32
  as channel for hostility, 49, 150-152
  as channel for other feelings, 48-49
  as childish play, 49
  components of, 48
  erotization, 48
  fight-flight reaction in, 49
  fused with jealousy, 49
  fused with love for mating, 49
  interest of youth in, 173

Index

and mating, 48
mature, 48-50
overinhibited, 49
as physiological mechanism, 48
rebellion against parents, 150-152
and sensualism, 48
Shakespeare, *Richard III*, 44, 170
Social forces, biological basis of, 187
Social influences on criminality, 77-78
Social motivation, 5
Social organization
  animal, 12
  human, 12
  influenced by childhood training, 57-58
Southard, Ernest, 181
Spanking, 176
Status
  in animal groups, 11
  wish for, 41
Stress
  marriage as, 106
  parenthood as, 106
  physiological reaction to, 13
  sociological, 59-61
Sublimation
  form of flight, 15
  of hostility, 69, 81, 114-117
  introduced by Freud, 114
"Success," definition of, 89-90, 171
Suicide, hostility in, 19
Superego, 30, 32
  analyzed and corrected in psychoanalytic treatment, 183
  as the biological tendency for social cooperation, 30
  and conscience, 30
  conscious, 90
  and imagos, 45
  product of parental conditioning and training, 45-47
  role in control of hostility, 66
  as source of hostility, 47, 102
  unconscious, 96
Superego, disorders, 46, 173-176
Suppression, 81
Survival, 2, 59-61
  human because of adaptability, 10
  of fittest, 10

Therapy, *See* Psychoanalytic treatment
Transference in psychoanalytic treatment, 183-186
Treatment, *See* Psychoanalytic treatment

Van Loon, Willem, *The Arts*, 65

War
  exclusive human group activity, 12
  history of, 65
  irrationality of, 196
  results of, 23
Withdrawal, in depressions, 19
"Withdrawal state"
  case of, 17, 18-19
  form of flight, 17-19

Zilboorg, Gregory, *Psychology of Criminal Acts*, 75